MARRIAGE: A COVENANT BEFORE GOD

10 PRINCIPLES FROM ADAM AND EVE TO ESTABLISH A MARRIAGE COVENANT GOD'S WAY

By
Pastor & Missionary Jeremy Markle

WALKING IN THE WORD MINISTRIES

Pastor/Missionary Jeremy Markle
www.walkinginthewordministries.net

Marriage: A Covenant Before God
*10 Principles from Adam and Eve
to Establish a Marriage Covenant God's Way*

All rights reserved solely by the author.
No part of this book may be reproduced, stored in a retrieval system, or transmitted in any form or by any means – electronic, mechanical, photocopy, recording, or otherwise – without written permission of the author.

Unless otherwise noted,
all Scripture quotations are from the King James Version.

Copyright © 2015 by Pastor Jeremy Markle.

Published by Walking in the WORD Ministries
www.walkinginthewordministries.net

Printed in the United States of America

ISBN: 978-0692498286

I wish to lovingly dedicate this book
to my wife, Laura,
who is my best friend and favorite companion.

Special Thank You

**To Joanna Lynch
for her help with both
gramatik review and graphic design.**

Table of Contents

Preface

My Prayer

Introduction

The CREATOR of the Marriage Covenant

Articles

I. The Commencement and Termination of the Marriage Covenant .... pg. 1
   - Biblical Principles Displayed in Common Wedding Traditions

II. The Preparations for the Marriage Covenant .... pg. 11
   - Walking Together In Harmony
   - Reestablishing Purity Following Promiscuity

III. The Significance of the Marriage Covenant .... pg. 29
   - Unifying Differences
   - The Necessity of Humility for True Unity

IV. The Roles in the Marriage Covenant .... pg. 39
   - Recognizing the Differences Between Men and Women
   - A Practical Understanding of Men & Women Based On Adam and Eve
   - Admirable Characteristics for a Life-Long Relationship as Displayed by Boaz and Ruth

V. The Responsibilities of the Marriage Covenant .... pg. 53
   - Reality of Responsibility
   - Reversal of Responsibility

VI. The Terms of the Marriage Covenant .... pg. 67
- 5 Levels of Communication
- The Significance of Friendship in the Marriage Covenant
- Biblical Pointers for Proper Communication

VII. The Conflicts in the Marriage Covenant .... pg. 77
- 5 Stages of Accepting New Things
- Keeping the Peace
- The Common Catalysts and Counsel for Marriage Conflict
- Discovering Differences
- Monthly Budgeting

VIII. The Restoration of the Marriage Covenant .... pg. 105
- Rekindling the Flame
- 11 Investments for Life-Long Love

IX. The Expansion of the Marriage Covenant .... pg. 121
- "My Son" Throughout Proverbs

X. The Fulfillment in the Marriage Covenant .... pg. 137
- Physical Intimacy Scale
- The P's of Proper Physical Intimacy
- What is Honorable in Marriage?
- Tips for Intimacy
- Illustrated Difference of Intimacy for a Man and a Woman
- Causes and Cures for Tension in Intimacy

Samples

Charge to the Couple
Wedding Vows
Marriage Certificate

Preface

A few years ago, while serving the Lord on the mission field, I received the joyous news that one of my beloved family members was going to be married. Then, to my pleasant surprise, I was asked to return home for a short visit so that I could officiate the wedding. After accepting the invitation, I realized the great responsibility I was undertaking by helping to establish a new home that would glorify God. So with a pastor's commitment to God's Word, and a family member's love, I began to search the Scriptures for the clearest example of Biblical matrimony this young couple could learn from and follow. My goal was to provide a solid foundation for their relationship before the wedding so that they would be prepared for the life God had for them. It was through that search that God led me back to the beginning--the beginning of man and woman, the beginning of marriage. For *"In the beginning ... God created man in his own image ... and ...made he a woman, and brought her unto the man"* (Genesis 1:1, 27, 2:22).

What I am now privileged to share with you is what I lovingly shared with those who are dear to me as they prepared to enter into a marriage covenant before God and man. These biblical truths are accompanied by practical illustrations and applications so that you and your loved one might grow in your knowledge of each other and God's will for your future together. **My prayer is that these studies and the additional material given will provide a solid foundation on which you can build a marriage and family that will be both personally satisfying as well as God-honoring until death do you part.**

Pastor Jeremy Markle

The CREATOR of the Marriage Covenant

God is the Creator of marriage, which started in the Garden of Eden. Genesis 2:18-25 provides us with God's plan for and provision of a perfect marriage between man and woman as it says, *"And the LORD God said, It is not good that the man should be alone; I will make him an help meet for him. And out of the ground the LORD God formed every beast of the field, and every fowl of the air; and brought them unto Adam to see what he would call them: and whatsoever Adam called every living creature, that was the name thereof. And Adam gave names to all cattle, and to the fowl of the air, and to every beast of the field; but for Adam there was not found an help meet for him. And the LORD God caused a deep sleep to fall upon Adam, and he slept: and he took one of his ribs, and closed up the flesh instead thereof; And the rib, which the LORD God had taken from man, made he a woman, and brought her unto the man. And Adam said, This is now bone of my bones, and flesh of my flesh: she shall be called Woman, because she was taken out of Man. Therefore shall a man leave his father and his mother, and shall cleave unto his wife: and they shall be one flesh. And they were both naked, the man and his wife, and were not ashamed."* On the sixth day of creation, Adam and Eve entered not only into a contract between themselves, but by having God being the witness to their marriage, they entered into a Spiritual Covenant with Him as well (Malachi 2:14, Proverbs

2:16-17). Malachi 2:14, while speaking of the marriage relationship says, *"... Because the LORD hath been witness between thee and the wife of thy youth ... yet is she thy companion, and the wife of thy covenant."*

Shortly following God's creation of Adam and Eve, and their becoming husband and wife, *"they heard the voice of the LORD God walking in the garden in the cool of the day"* (Genesis 3:8). God had not only created man and women for each other, He also created them to have a personal relationship with Him. Sadly, due to the shame of their sin, Adam and Eve *"hid themselves from the presence of the LORD God amongst the trees of the garden"* (Genesis 3:8). Adam and Eve had individually sinned against God, and their relationship with Him was affected. Thankfully, God, lovingly confronted Adam and Eve with their disobedience, and, although the consequences of sin sorrow, pain, and death could not be removed, God did offer His forgiveness and personal provision of *"coats of skins, and clothed them"* (Genesis 3:21, Romans 6:23). God's permanent solution for sin was also pronounced as He cursed the serpent by saying, *"I will put enmity between thee and the woman, and between thy seed and her seed; it shall bruise thy head, and thou shalt bruise his heel"* (Genesis 3:15). God's prophecy about the seed of a women was fulfilled in the virgin birth of Jesus Christ (Matthew 1:20-25). While speaking of Mary, the mother of Jesus, Matthew 1:21 says, *"And she shall bring forth a son, and thou shalt call his name JESUS: for he shall save his people from their sins."* Jesus Christ came *"to seek and to save that which was lost"* (Luke 19:10). He came to restore the broken relationship that sin has caused between mankind and God by paying for all of mankind's sin on the cross of Calvary and making His payment freely available to all those who personally believe on Him (I John 2:1-2).

Each young couple that desires to have a close and loving relationship together must first individually have a personal relationship with God the Father through Jesus Christ (John 14:6). They must recognize that they are sinners and have *"come short of the glory of God*" (Romans 3:23). Then they must personally accept God's gift of forgiveness by believing in the death, burial and resurrection of Jesus Christ as the only adequate payment for their sin (Romans 6:23, 10:9-10, Ephesians 2:8-9, I Corinthians 15:1-4). *"For God so loved the world, that he gave his only begotten Son, that whosoever believeth in him should not perish, but have everlasting life"* (John 3:16). After the bride and groom have personally experienced God's love and have a restored personal relationship with Him, they can truly begin to love each other. I John 4:10-12 explains by saying, *"Herein is love, not that we loved God, but that he loved us, and sent his Son to be the propitiation for our sins. Bloved, if God so loved us, we ought also to love one another. No man hath seen God at any time. If we love one another, God dwelleth in us, and his love is perfected in us."* God's personal love for the bride and groom must be their example of how to love each other in their Marriage Covenant. Just as they must receive God's expressed sacrificial love through Jesus Christ, so they must receive their spouse's sacrificial love and learn to express their love for their spouse sacrificially.

Those couples who desire God's continued blessing and presence on their wedding day and throughout their marriage must look to God for His teaching and guidance found in His Word for every aspect of their relationship. They must learn and follow their God-given roles and responsibilities before God and man. As the Marriage Covenant is proclaimed by the pastor's declaration of, "in the presence of God and these witnesses, I pronounce you husband and wife," a covenant has been made which should never be broken. It is therefore, important that both parties preparing to join in such a covenant are fully aware of what God says about marriage. Ecclesiastes 5:2-6 warns, *"Be not rash with thy mouth, and let not thine heart be hasty to utter any thing before God: for God is in heaven, and thou upon earth: therefore let thy words be few ... When thou vowest a vow unto God, defer not to pay it; for he hath no pleasure in fools: pay that which thou hast vowed. Better is it that thou shouldest not vow, than that thou shouldest vow and not pay. Suffer not thy mouth to cause thy flesh to sin; neither say thou before the angel, that it was an error: wherefore should God be angry at thy voice, and destroy the work of thine hands?"*

Unfortunately many young couples believe that marriage is nothing more than "dating" while living in the same house. They don't take seriously the need for Godly preparation and counsel. For this reason they are spending the first months and years of the matrimony struggling to find out how it all works. This is similar to a parent giving his 16 year old child with the keys to the new family car without providing him with any textbook and hands on training. The reasons could be provided; he has driven bumping cars before (dated), or he has been in a family car and watched his parents drive all his life. But neither of these past experiences are true preparation grounds nor do they guarantee that the experience gained was truly correct. They can not replace the need for a text book to learn the rules and personal guidance to gain the experience. God does not desire his children to jump into the driver's seat of marriage, only to crash. For this reason God has revealed His pattern for a proper marriage throughout His Word. Therefore, it is the goal of this study to use the first marriage found in Genesis 2 and 3 as well as other Biblical passages to prepare you for one of the most important and permanent decisions of your life.

Chapter 1

Article I
The Commencement and Termination of the Marriage Covenant
Genesis 2:18-24

The Commencement of the Marriage Covenant

God's timing is always precise. He has a reason for every change and delay to man's plans (Proverbs 16:9). The timing of Adam and Eve's marriage was not an exception. Genesis 2:18 reveals Adam's condition before his "wedding." God said, ***"It is not good that the man should be alone; I will make him an help meet for him."*** God recognized Adam's need for a wife, but He did not bring about an immediate resolution. Verses 19-20 reveal some responsibilities Adam needed to be complete before God could provide him with his needed wife.

As Adam followed God's leading to take charge of the Garden of Eden (vrs. 15) and name the animals, he fulfilled his spiritual (obedience to God) and physical (preparation of a home) responsibilities. Perhaps, God knew that Adam would never finish naming all the animals after he saw and experienced the presence of Eve? The same is true for a Christian couple desiring to get married today. There may be some specific tasks God desires to do in and through them before they are joined in matrimony. I Corinthians 7:33-34 say, ***"But he that is married careth for the things that are of the world, how he may please his wife. There is difference also between a wife and a virgin. The unmarried woman careth for the things of the Lord, that she may be holy both in body and in spirit: but she that is married careth for the things of the world, how she may please her husband."*** Time spent in singleness is not wasted, but rather "invested" in greater opportunities to serve God (Mary and Joseph - Matthew 1:18-25).

As a Christian couple considers the timing of their wedding, they must consider all that God desires for them to accomplish and have accomplished in them before their wedding. Psalm 37:4 and 5 say, *"Delight thyself also in the LORD; and he shall give thee the desires of thine heart. Commit thy way unto the LORD; trust also in him; and he shall bring it to pass."* An impulsive couple who rushes to the alter because of "love" or any other reason and who have neglected to take the time to pray and wait for specific answers to their prayers are in great danger of stepping into their marriage relationship outside of God's will and without God's blessing. Philippians 4:6 and 7 say, *"Be careful for nothing; but in every thing by prayer and supplication with thanksgiving let your requests be made known unto God. And the peace of God, which passeth all understanding, shall keep your hearts and minds through Christ Jesus."* Impulsiveness or impatience shows a lack of patience–patience which provides the maturity needed for a Christian matrimony.

James 1:2-4 expresses it this way, *"My brethren, count it all joy when ye fall into divers temptations; knowing this, that the trying of your faith worketh patience. But let patience have her perfect work, that ye may be perfect and entire, wanting nothing."* In the progression of a relationship, there are many temptations to move faster than God desires. These temptations provide opportunities to practice patience. The lack of patience or flexibility during the dating relationship, or an overabundance of frustration and irritation during the engagement and wedding planning, all reveal a fleshly rebellion against God's timing and authority. However, by the practice of godly patience through each stage of the relationship, the couple becomes more dependent on God and becomes more prepared in their spiritual maturity for the new life they are starting together. If they skip this important process, they are showing their lack of maturity, and are missing out on some of the priceless maturing lessons

♥The Commencement and Termination of the Marriage Covenant♥

God wants them to learn so that they will be the best husband and wife they can be for each other for the rest of their lives.

♥ *Have we truly taken time to pray and ask God for His will and direction in our wedding and marriage plans, including the date we have chosen?*

♥ *Have we waited long enough to be able to see specific answers to our prayers to assure us of God's blessing on our plans?*

♥ *Are we willing to change our plans and even our wedding date if God begins to show us these changes need to be made by way of circumstances or Godly counsel?*

The Termination of the Marriage Covenant

A husband and wife are declared to be "one flesh" in Genesis 2:24 which says, **"*Therefore shall a man leave his father and his mother, and shall cleave unto his wife: and they shall be one flesh.*"** Jesus Christ uses this same statement to provide God's view of the permanency of marriage in Matthew 19:3-6. It says, **"*The Pharisees also came unto him, tempting him, and saying unto him, Is it lawful for a man to put away his wife for every cause? And he answered and said unto them, Have ye not read, that he which made them at the beginning made them male and female, and said, For this cause shall a man leave father and mother, and shall cleave to his wife: and they twain shall be one flesh? Wherefore they are no more twain, but one flesh. What therefore God hath joined together, let not man put asunder.*"** The joining of two individuals in the Marriage Covenant by God is to be permanent. Jesus Christ is very clear to those looking for an excuse to divorce their spouse when He says, **"*What therefore God hath joined together, let not man put*** *asunder."* God has authored the Marriage Covenant in such a way that the only proper way to terminate the agreement is through death. For a Christian couple, the only pre-nuptial agreement they should consider is their Last Will and Testimony. I Corinthians 7:39 says, ***"The wife is bound by the law as long as her husband liveth; but if her husband be dead, she is at liberty to be married to whom she will; only in the Lord."*** and Romans 7:2-3 agrees by saying, ***"For the woman which hath an husband is bound by the law to her husband so long as he liveth; but if the husband be dead, she is loosed from the law of her husband. So then if, while her husband liveth, she be married to another man, she shall be called an adulteress: but if her husband be dead, she is free from that law; so that she is no adulteress, though she be married to another man."*** There must not be any doubt on this very important claim to God's authority over the Marriage Covenant. God's plan for marriage is "until death do us part!"

❤ *Are we committed to God's plan for marriage to be "until death do us part?"*

❥Relationship Building Questions❥
Article I

1. Are we presently, as singles, fulfilling our spiritual and physical responsibilities in our lives?
    a. List a few spiritual responsibilities outside of your relationship which you currently are fulfilling:
        i. _____
        ii. _____
        iii. _____
    b. List a few physical responsibilities outside of your relationship which you currently are fulfilling:
        i. _____
        ii. _____
        iii. _____

2. Have we spent time together and separately in prayer asking God for His will and timing in our wedding plans? _____
   How has God answered our prayers up to this point in our planning process?
    a. _____
    b. _____
    c. _____
    d. _____

3. How have we shown patience and individually matured by waiting for God's direction and provision in our relationship?
    a. _____
    b. _____
    c. _____
    d. _____

4. Are we both committed to follow through with our Marriage Covenant "until death do us part?" _____

Biblical Principles Displayed in Common Wedding Traditions

- **The seating of the parents** - The couple is honoring the authority and role of their parents in their relationship by giving them a prominent position as they make their covenant together (Genesis 24:1-67, Ephesians 6:2)
- **The positioning of the groom** - The groom is waiting for his bride to be brought to him just as Adam waited for God to bring Eve (Genesis 2:21-22)
- **The entrance of the bride with her father** - The father is displaying his protection and leadership over his daughter and his willingness to relinquish his role to the groom (Numbers 30:3-16)
- **The bride dressed in all white** - The bride is displaying her moral and physical purity as she presents herself to her groom (Revelation 19:7-8)

- **The pastor's leadership over the ceremony** - The pastor's role displays the couple's desire for God to be the officiating authority over their marriage and their recognition of the church's involvement in their home (Matthew 19:4-6, Mark 10:6-9, Hebrews 10:24, 13:7, 13)
- **The spiritual challenge to the couple** - The spiritual challenge establishes a pattern for the couple to always follow God's instruction for their relationship (Ephesians 5:22-33, Colossians 3:18-19)
- **The exchange of vows** - The verbal exchange of the vows, in God's house, in God's presence, and before human witnesses, reveals the bride's and groom's permanent covenant together as husband and wife for the rest of their lives (Ruth 4:1-12, Ecclesiastes 5:1-7, Matthew 19:6, Mark 10:9)
- **The exchanging of rings** - The giving and receiving of rings as gifts is an expression of the bride's and groom's commitment to enter into their marriage covenant, and displays their delight to share their earthly possessions (Genesis 24:51-53, Ruth 4:7, Ephesians 5:33)
    - The rings' circular shape is a reminder that their love must be unending (I Corinthians 13:2-8a)
    - The rings' creation out of costly metal (gold) displays that they are willing sacrifice for their love (John 15:11, I Corinthians 7:33-34)
    - The rings' continual presence on their fingers is a reminder to them of their covenant of love and the authority of love they must abide by even when they are a great distance apart (Matthew 19:6, Mark 10:9, I Corinthians 13:8a)

- **The pronouncement of the couple** - The pastoral pronouncement of the couple as "man and wife" officially establishes that a public covenant has been made and that the bride and groom are officially joined together until death do they part (Genesis 2:23-24, Matthew 19:5-6, Mark 10:7-8, Ephesians 5:31)
- **The lifting of the veil and kiss** - The veil being lifted by the groom displays his privileged right to reveal the bride's beauty, and by kissing her he expresses that he will find his satisfaction in her beauty alone, while the bride displays her willingness and welcoming of the grooms authority and partaking of her beauty (Genesis 2:25, Proverbs 5:15-19, Song of Solomon 4:9-11)
- **The lighting of the unity candle** - The lighting of the singular candle from two pre-lit candles displays the new one flesh relationship, the bride and groom have begun (Genesis 2:24, Matthew 19:5-6, Mark 10:7-8, Ephesians 5:31)
- **The presentation of the couple** - The public pronouncement of the couple by name establishes that the bride and groom are no longer to be known as children of their parents, or from separate families, but as one new family (Genesis 2:23, Matthew 19:5-6, Mark 10:7-8, Ephesians 5:31)
- **The wedding reception** - The couple has the opportunity to work together as husband and wife to host their first reception of their family and friends as they all celebrate their new life together (Matthew 22:1-14, Revelation 19:7-9)

Chapter 2

Article II
The Preparations for the Marriage Covenant
Genesis 2:18, 21-22, 24-25

The Marriage must be According to God's will

God is seen throughout the entire process of Adam and Eve's marriage. Genesis 2:18 reports, **"And the LORD God said."** Genesis 2:21 continues with **"And the LORD God caused"** and Genesis 2:22 finishes with, **"the LORD God ... made ... and brought her unto the man."** God should be just as involved in any Christian young couple's preparation for marriage. God should have the "say" as to the true need for marriage. He should be trusted to guide life's circumstances for the couple to meet, and He should be waited on for the final provision for and joining of the bride and groom to make their Marriage Covenant together. Psalm 127:1 says, **"Except the LORD build the house, they labour in vain that build it ..."**

Unfortunately, God is left out of marriage preparation when the motives for marriage are based on man's counsel of who is the correct spouse and on man's inventions to bring about the meeting of a spouse. For this reason, each prospective mate must make sure that he/she is getting married for the right reason and in the right way. First, it is very dangerous for a guy or girl to get married in order to escape their parents, home, or loneliness, fulfill social obligations, finances, or cover guilt due to sin (Matthew 1:18-25). Second, it is very dangerous to get married because of "attraction" (Judges 14:1-3). It is very interesting to note that as Adam spoke of Eve, he never mentioned her beauty. Do not misunderstand, God has made each man and each woman with personal tastes of who and what they consider beautiful, and He desires them to be pleased with and attracted to whomever they are going to share the rest of our lives. But, Proverbs 31:30 is clear, *"Favour is deceitful, and beauty is vain: but a woman [man] that feareth the LORD, she [he] shall be praised."* Third, it is very dangerous for a guy or girl to get married because of sensual passion or lust (Judges 16:1-3). Although sensual passion should be expressed in marriage, and although marriage is a protection from sexual sins (I Corinthians 7:1-9), marriage is much more than an easy license to quickly enjoy fleshly pleasure. Paul's warning to Timothy, a young man, must be applied to the lives of every young person when he says, *"Flee also youthful lusts ..."* (II Timothy 2:22). Fourth, it is very dangerous for a guy or girl to get married because of emotion or "love" (Judges 16:4-6). The world's idea of love is directly contrary to God's. The world says love is an *emotion* that makes *me feel good*. But God says love is *my choice* to *do good for the individual loved.* *"Charity [LOVE] suffereth long, and is kind; charity envieth not; charity vaunteth not itself, is not puffed up, doth not behave itself unseemly, seeketh not her own, is not easily provoked, thinketh no evil; rejoiceth not in iniquity, but rejoiceth in the truth; beareth all things, believeth all things, hopeth all things, endureth all things. Charity never faileth ..."* (I Corinthians 13:4-8). Biblical *"Love worketh no ill to his neighbour ..."* (Romans 13:10). Therefore, true love will never encourage another individual to commit sin or make a decision which is not truly in their best interest. When a couple desires to get married because they have seen God lead them together so that they can commit their lives to the service of their partner, they are prepared for the Marriage Covenant.

❤ Have we seen God's hand throughout our lives to bring us to this point of being joined in the Marriage Covenant?
❤ Are we committed to truly love each other according to God's idea of love?

♥The Preparations for the Marriage Covenant♥

The Marriage must be Based on the Approval of God-given Human Authority

God established a fundamental standard for the parent-child relationship as He said, *"Therefore shall a man leave his father and his mother, and shall cleave unto his wife: and they shall be one flesh"* (Genesis 2:24, Matthew 19:4-6). The word "therefore" connects an event to the cause for the event. The event was the separation of the parent-child relationship. The reason for the event was that the man and woman were beginning a new unique life, separated not from the *influence* of, but from the *authority* of their parents (Exodus 18:1-27, Mark 7:10). The significance of this statement is overwhelming. Adam and Eve never had parents, and they never had been parents. The role of a parent had not yet existed in the history of mankind. But God, from the very first marriage, wanted to establish the extension of parental authority until the Marriage Covenant. A couple who makes plans for marriage outside of their parents' approval and counsel is at great risk of being in direct rebellion against God (Ephesians 6:1-3). In addition to parental authority, throughout history and the revelation of His Word, God has provided government and church authorities over couples as well (Romans 13:1-7, Ephesians 4:11-17, Hebrews 13:7, 17). If each of these authorities are not considered and heeded, the couple will find themselves outside of God's safety and blessing. Proverbs 11:14 speaks clearly, *"Where no counsel is, the people fall: but in the multitude of counsellors there is safety."* A marriage built without counsel, or which rejects proper counsel, will find itself in ruin. In contrast, the marriage which welcomes God-given counsel will be a refuge from danger.

♥ *Have we honored our God-given authorities and godly counsel as we pursue our marriage relationship?*

❤The Preparations for the Marriage Covenant❤

❤ *Are we willing to continue to seek godly counsel and instruction for our marriage now and in the future?*

The Marriage must be Prepared for According to God's Word

God's standard for choosing a mate for the Marriage Covenant

In the area of choosing the correct spouse, Adam and Eve had an advantage because God was their matchmaker, but their relationship still provides guiding principles. Genesis 2:22 says God made **"*a woman, and brought her unto the man.*"** God specifically created and chose the exact woman Adam needed. Adam did not have any choice in the matter, and he did not need to go about searching on his own. God was the initiator of the relationship and the match was perfect. To help protect His children from making wrong choices in their marriage partners, God has provided one specific standard for all those wanting to be married. II Corinthians 6:14 says, **"*Be ye not unequally yoked together with unbelievers: for what fellowship hath righteousness with unrighteousness? and what communion hath light with darkness?*"** The idea of being "yoked together" is to be joined together for the same purpose, including, but not limited to, an official agreement. Amos 3:3 asks an important question for each human relationship including marriage by saying, **"*Can two walk together, except they be agreed?*"**

It is very important that both parties preparing to sign the Marriage Covenant are equal in their relationship with God (II Corinthians 6:14-18). They must both be one of God's children, having followed the pattern established in John 1:12 as it says, **"*But as many as received him, to them gave he power to become*"** *the sons of God, even to them that believe on his name."* They must both have believed on or trusted en Jesus Christ as their personal Savior by expressing their faith in the Biblical fact *"that Christ died for our sins according to the scriptures; And that he was buried, and that he rose again the third day according to the scriptures"* (I Corinthians 15:1-4). Ephesians 2:8-9 explains further by saying, *"For by grace are ye saved through faith; and that not of yourselves: it is the gift of God: Not of works, lest any man should boast."* Each party must have a spiritual birth day in which they accepted God's gift of eternal life through Jesus Christ's payment for their sin (John 3:1-18, I John 2:1-2). Then, they must both be equally dedicated to living for God by obeying His Word and will in every area of their life and family, or they will be violating God's plan for their marriage before they get started (John 15:7-8,).

Malachi 2:11-12 presents the standard for marriage by saying, *"Judah hath dealt treacherously, and an abomination is committed in Israel and in Jerusalem; for Judah hath profaned the holiness of the LORD which he loved, and hath married the daughter of a strange god. The LORD will cut off the man that doeth this ..."* II Corinthians 6:17 and 18 command, *"Wherefore come out from among them, and be ye separate, saith the Lord, and touch not the unclean thing; and I will receive you, and will be a Father unto you, and ye shall be my sons and daughters, saith the Lord Almighty."* When a believer separates himself from a close relationship with the world and the unsaved, God promises him a closer relationship with Himself, a relationship which can never be compared to any earthly relationship. This close relationship with God must never be sacrificed for a temporal relationship in marriage (Luke 14:26-27).

❤ *Have we both shared our salvation testimony with our potential spouse?*

♥The Preparations for the Marriage Covenant♥

♥ *Are we both committed to live for God before and after our wedding, putting Him first in all things?*

God's standard of staying pure
until the Marriage Covenant

In the area of purity, Adam and Eve had another advantage over present-day relationships. They did not have the years of temptation and the conflict with their flesh. Sin had not yet entered their world. Yet the Biblical disclosure of their relationship helps reveal God's plan for a man and woman's physical relationship. Genesis 2:24 says, **"and they shall be one flesh."** God was declaring that the sexual one flesh relationship was enjoyed only after Marriage Covenant was made, following the "I do." Verse 25 goes on to say, **"And they were both naked, the man and his wife, and were not ashamed."** Nakedness or physical intimacy outside of the Marriage Covenant always brings shame (I Samuel 13:11-17).

The Bible is very clear about the importance of purity between a man and woman before marriage. God's Word calls physical intimacy before the signing of the Marriage Covenant, **"fornication"** (I Corinthians 6:13-20). A young couple will be tempted by the world, your flesh, and the Devil with this specific sin. The world says that physical intimacy must be experienced or a couple will not know if they will be happy together. The flesh constantly desires pleasure now, even if it is only short-lived, and causes long-term damage (Hebrews 11:25b). The Devil knows that physical intimacy in marriage is God's perfect will, and he wants to destroy anything good God has planned for you in the future. Proverbs 22:3, and 27:12 both say, **"A prudent man foreseeth the evil, and hideth himself: but the simple pass on, and are punished."** Couples must realize the danger of being physically intimate before marriage. Paul gave counsel for this difficult temptation in I Corinthians 7:1, which says, **"Now

❤The Preparations for the Marriage Covenant❤

concerning the things whereof ye wrote unto me: It is good for a man not to touch a woman." The couple should follow Joseph's example of resisting temptation to be intimate until the Marriage Covenant is signed. He responded, *"how then can I do this great wickedness, and sin against God"* (Genesis 39:9b)? And when Potiphar's wife *"caught him by his garment, saying, Lie with me: and he left his garment in her hand, and fled, and got him out"* (Genesis 39:12). I Corinthians 6:18 speaks plainly on the subject, *"Flee fornication. Every sin that a man doeth is without the body; but he that committeth fornication sinneth against his own body."* Solomon provides counsel to his son about this subject in a very vivid manner in Proverbs 6:26-29 which says, *"For the commandment is a lamp; and the law is light; and reproofs of instruction are the way of life: to keep thee from the evil woman, from the flattery of the tongue of a strange woman. Lust not after her beauty in thine heart; neither let her take thee with her eyelids. Can a man take fire in his bosom, and his clothes not be burned? Can one go upon hot coals, and his feet not be burned? So he that goeth in to his neighbour's wife; whosoever toucheth her shall not be innocent."* Paul realized that his solution was a temporary fix to a life long temptation. He gave a final solution in I Corinthians 7:2-5 when he said, *"Nevertheless, to avoid fornication, let every man have his own wife, and let every woman have her own husband ..."*

❤ Have we already set, and will we continue to set Godly protection in our relationship so that we will enter our marriage as pure vessels and enjoy God's approval on our physical intimacy?

❧Relationship Building Questions❦
Article II

1. Why are we getting married? _____
   _____
   _____
   _____

2. What are some examples of how God has been a part of bringing us to this point in our relationship?
   a. _____
   b. _____
   c. _____
   d. _____
   e. _____

3. Are we committed to biblically love each other, sacrificially, for the rest of our lives? _____

4. From whom have we sought counsel and received approval for our relationship?
   a. _____
   b. _____
   c. _____
   d. _____
   e. _____

5. Are we committed to make sure that every step we take closer to our wedding vows is in submission to God and our authorities? _____

6. Have we ever shared our personal salvation testimony in detail with each other? _____

♥The Preparations for the Marriage Covenant♥

7. Are we both committed, presently as singles, and in the future as a couple, to encourage each other to grow in the knowledge of and service to our Lord, Jesus Christ? _____
   _____

8. Are we maintaining our physical purity until our wedding day? _____

9. What protective measures have we taken to ensure that we get to the wedding altar pure?
   a. _____
   b. _____
   c. _____
   d. _____
   e. _____

Walking Together In Harmony

Amos 3:3
Can two walk together, except they be agreed?

A man and a woman who desire to live in harmony together must be in agreement about the most important decisions of their lives. Therefore, they must openly and thoroughly discuss their personal beliefs about Who God is and what role His Word will play in their home. They must be willing to share their personal testimony of how they have accepted the Lord Jesus Christ as their personal Savior as well as any other spiritual commitments they may have made to obey His will for their future. They must recognize that they, as one flesh, cannot "**serve two masters**" (Luke 16:13). And therefore, each of these topics must be discussed with open hearts and minds so as to verify that they are truly in agreement in order that they can "**walk together**" in harmony for the rest of their lives. If they find that their beliefs about God, His Word or His will differ, they must consider the possibility that God was allowing their paths to cross for a time but that it is not His perfect will for them to make a commitment to "**walk together**" until death doth they part.

With regards to pursuing a marriage in which one of the parties does not have a testimony of accepting Jesus Christ as their personal Savior, and thereby not being a child of God, the Bible is clear, "**Be ye not unequally yoked together with unbelievers: for what fellowship hath righteousness with unrighteousness? and what communion hath light with darkness? ...**" (II Corinthians 6:14-18). The concept of yoking two animals together is logical and simple. By joining two animals together, the workload would be lessened, and the outcome of the labor would be more reliable as they both walk the same path together. However, if two kinds of animals, or two animals with completely different temperaments, abilities, etc., where joined together, the work load would be increased, and the outcome unreliable because they would constantly seek to walk in different directions and at different speeds (Deuteronomy 22:10). In the same way, God says that His followers should not join themselves to those who are not walking the same path of faith in God (Matthew 7:13-14, Exodus 34:14-16, I Kings 11:4). Deuteronomy 7:4 warns that the joining of a believer and an unbeliever will cause devastating results, "*For they will turn away thy son from following me, that they may serve other gods: so will the anger of the LORD be kindled against you, and destroy thee suddenly.*"

Abraham understood this principle thousands of years before it was articulated. That is why he asked his most trusted servant to "*... swear by the LORD, the God of heaven, and the God of the earth, that thou shalt not take a wife unto my son of the daughters of the Canaanites, among whom I dwell: But thou shalt go unto my country, and to my kindred, and take a wife unto my son Isaac*" (Genesis 24:3-4). But Abraham's desire was not limited to the girl's belief in the same God: he required that she have the same level of faith and obedience as well. Abraham had to trust God by leaving his family and homeland, and his wife Sarah followed his leadership. Now, Isaac's wife would need to make the same choice by faith. She would need to display her willingness to leave all in obedience to God's will for her life and future marriage by faith. Then Abraham's servant, knowing that this level of faith and obedience is not easy to find, asked, "*Peradventure the woman will not be willing to follow me unto this land: must I needs bring thy son again unto the land from whence thou camest?*" (Genesis 24:5). And Abraham's answer was clear, "*Beware thou that thou bring not my son thither again*" (Genesis 24:6). Although such a requirement was high, Abraham understood that it was needed. He wanted the best for his son, and he believed God would provide it, so he reassured his servant by saying, "***The LORD God of heaven, which took me from my father's house, and from the land of my kindred, and which spake unto me, and that sware unto me, saying, Unto thy seed will I give this land; he shall send his angel before thee, and thou shalt take a wife unto my son from thence***" (Genesis 24:7). Knowing the possible temptation for his servant to make an exception to his wishes in order to fulfill his oath, he goes on to free him of any responsibility or shame by saying, "***And if the woman will not be willing to follow thee, then thou shalt be clear from this my oath: only bring not my son thither again***" (Genesis 24:8). Abraham was not so desperate for a wife for Isaac that he was willing to lower his standards because of the fear that God would not provide the "perfect" mate in His perfect timing. **He did not just desire a "good" girl for his son. He demanded a "godly" girl for his son.**

A couple "in love" must make sure that they are not being led by their flesh. "***For he that soweth to his flesh shall of the flesh reap corruption ...***" (Galatians 6:8). They must be willing to set aside their "emotional love" for each other so that they might "think soberly" about the life-long commitment they are making together (Titus 2:4, 6). They must choose to "spiritually love" each other by making sure that their present actions and future plans will not lead either one of them away from a close walk with God and into sin. (Romans 13:10).

I John 2:15-17

15 Love not the world,
neither the things that are in the world.
If any man love the world,
the love of the Father is not in him.
16 For all that is in the world,
the lust of the flesh,
and the lust of the eyes,
and the pride of life,
is not of the Father, but is of the world.
17 And the world passeth away, and the lust thereof:
but he that doeth the will of God abideth for ever.

Joshua 24:15

And if it seem evil unto you to serve the LORD,
choose you this day whom ye will serve;
... but as for me and my house, we will serve the LORD.

Dear friend,
the termination of a precious relationship is never easy.
But consider how much more devastating
would be the destruction of a marriage
because it was not in agreement about
God, His Word, and a personal relationship with Him
from the beginning.
Relinquish the control of your desires and dreams
to your loving Heavenly Father
Who promises to provide what is best for you
in accordance to His great love and perfect wisdom
so that you can truly enjoy
all that He has planned for you
since our creation.

Reestablishing Purity Following Promiscuity
II Samuel 11:1-12:24

- ✓ Recognize the steps leading to promiscuity (11:1-4)
  - The wrong place at the wrong time (1-2a)
    *Proverbs 7:7-10
    - → He was alone
    - → He was not in his proper place
    - → He was out late at night
  - The wrong look in the wrong direction (2b)
    *Matthew 5:27-28
    Lingering looks make lasting impressions
  - The wrong interest in the wrong person (3)
    *Exodus 20:17
  - The wrong request with the wrong intention (4a)
  - The wrong closeness with the wrong person (4b)
    *I Corinthians 7:1

- ✓ Recognize the short term pleasure of promiscuity (11:4c)
  *Hebrews 11:25

- ✓ Recognize the results of promiscuity (11:5-27, 12:1-23)
  *Psalm 32:3-4
  *I Corinthians 6:18-20
  - The chastity lost (illegitimate conception) (5)
    *James 1:13-15
  - The coverup (6-27)
  - The confrontation (12:1-9)

- ✂ The consequences (12:10-23)
  - → The personal punishment
    - ✎ Personal (10-11)
    - ✎ Family (15-23)
  - → The public humiliation (12)

✓ Recognize the need for confession after promiscuity (12:13a)
*Psalm 32:5a, 51:1-14

✓ Recognize the forgiveness for promiscuity (12:13b)
*Psalm 32:1-2, 5b

✓ Recognize the protection from promiscuity (12:24)
*Remove yourself from the situation in the fear of God - Genesis 39:7-16
*Establish a proper relationship by entering into a life-long marriage covenant - I Corinthians 7:1-5

John 8:1-11
*They say unto him,
Master, this woman was taken in adultery,
... what sayest thou? ... go, and sin no more.*

Chapter 3

Article III
The Significance of the Marriage Covenant
Marital Identity
Genesis 2:18-25, 3:20

The New Single Identity

Genesis 2:24 says, ***"Therefore shall a man leave his father and his mother, and shall cleave unto his wife: and they shall be one flesh."*** The one flesh relationship is much more than just physical intimacy. It is permanent unity. The "one flesh" relationship is the melding together of two lives to make one brand new and uniquely created individual entity. The husband and wife are to separate themselves from their previous family relationships so that they can form a new family unit. The husband and wife are now to cleave or be glued together with an inseparable bond. Their "new" identities are caught up in each other in the life long commitment made in the Marriage Covenant.

❤ *Are we ready to give up our individual identities for a new unified identity?*

The Single Identity Crisis

This new identity can cause identity confusion and crisis if viewed incorrectly. The world constantly teaches that each individual is to be his/her own man or woman and that he/she must look out for himself/herself. This is directly contrary to

God's Word and Will for the marriage relationship. First, the creation of man and woman in Genesis 2:18-25 helps to clarify God's view of the husband's and wife's mutual identity. Verse 18 says, *"And the LORD God said, It is not good that the man should be alone; I will make him an help meet for him."* God is very clear that, without Eve, Adam was in a unfinished condition. Although all the rest of creation was *"good,"* Adam was still not finished and said to be *"good"* until his life and identity were completed by Eve. Verses 21 and 22 say, *"And the LORD God caused a deep sleep to fall upon Adam, and he slept: and he took one of his ribs, and closed up the flesh instead thereof; And the rib, which the LORD God had taken from man, made he a woman, and brought her unto the man."* God specifically created Eve out of Adam's very "flesh and bone." Without Adam, Eve would not have been formed and would have no life or identity. For this reason, *"Adam said, she shall be called Woman, because she was taken out of Man"* (Genesis 2:23).

Adam, realizing the unity which God desired for them by creating Eve from his own rib, said, *"This is now bone of my bones, and flesh of my flesh"* (Genesis 2:23). Second, the scar on Adam's side from where God surgically *"took one of his ribs, and closed up the flesh instead thereof"* served as a constant reminder of their unity (Genesis 2:21). Third, Adam expressed their unity again by identifying himself with her when he extended his name from "man" to *"Woman, because she was taken out of Man"* (Genesis 2:23). Later, Adam again shows his authority to name his wife as he *"called his wife's name Eve; because she was the mother of all living"* (Genesis 2:20). Eve's first name, woman, indicated their unity in creation and matrimony, and her second name, Eve, indicated their unity by producing children through the *"one flesh"* relationship (Genesis 2:23, 3:20). Finally, although Adam and Eve never had parents or any other identity outside of God's knowledge of them, Adam authoritatively stated, *"Therefore shall a man leave his father and his mother, and shall cleave unto his wife: and they shall be one flesh"* (Genesis 2:24).

In a Biblically-based Marriage Covenant there is no identity crisis. Each party understands that they are separate from any other relationships for the purpose of being joined together with each other in a totally new and better relationship. They are totally secure in their understanding that God specifically created each of them for the other as well as for the roles they have in their new relationship. And they focus their lives on accomplishing each responsibility to the best of their ability.

❤ *Are we prepared to separate ourselves from our family and friends so that we can be totally dedicated to our new identity together?*

The Single Identity in Practice

"And Adam said, This is now bone of my bones, and flesh of my flesh ..." (Genesis 2:23). He recognized the direct connection between himself and his new wife. Their identities were together, and what happened to one would affect both of them. Sadly, this was illustrated in the fall of Adam and Eve as they ate of the fruit and were both punished together for their sin (Genesis 3:1-24). Their unified identity meant that they were unified both physically and spiritually (I Peter 3:7). This truth is also found in Ephesians 5:28 and 29 where instruction is given to the husband. It says, **"So ought men to love their wives as their own bodies. He that loveth his wife loveth himself. For no man ever yet hated his own flesh; but nourisheth and cherisheth it ..."**

The relationship of husband and wife is so close that whatever is done for one member of the relationship is done for the other

♥The Significance of the Marriage Covenant♥

as well (Proverbs 31:10-12, 23). One individual's achievements and rewards are extended to both of them. Proverbs illustrates this principle while speaking about the blessing of a good wife and the cursing of a bad wife in Proverbs 12:4 which says, ***"A virtuous woman is a crown to her husband: but she that maketh ashamed is as rottenness in his bones."*** Just as Adam and Eve shared the Garden of Eden, so in the Marriage Covenant what is the husband's becomes the wife's and what is the wife's becomes the husband's (I Corinthians 7:3-4). There is no division of possessions. Their identities and lives are universally connected. For this reason, at the wedding, the bride and groom commit "to love and to hold, from this day forward, for better for worse, for richer for poorer, in sickness and in health, to love and to cherish till death us do part."

♥ *Are we ready to make decisions together and live with the consequences together?*

♥ *Are we ready to have our spouse make decisions for us and live out the consequences, not matter what they may be?*

❧Relationship Building Questions❦
Article III

1. What will your new name be, based on your new identity?
    a. Groom: _____
    b. Bride: _____
    *Does it bother you that your name may change? _____
    *What are some companies or authorities who you need to contact because of your marriage?

Groom		Bride	
Vehicle Title	❑	SS	❑
_____	❑	_____	❑
_____	❑	_____	❑
_____	❑	_____	❑
_____	❑	_____	❑

2. Make a list of those individuals who are family and friends and who are very close to you.

Groom		Bride	
_____	❑	_____	❑
_____	❑	_____	❑
_____	❑	_____	❑
_____	❑	_____	❑
_____	❑	_____	❑

    *Are you prepared to separate yourself from these individuals so that you can be unified with your spouse? If yes, check the box.

♥The Significance of the Marriage Covenant♥

3. What are some decisions which your future spouse might make which make you nervous?
   a. _____
   b. _____
   c. _____
   d. _____
   e. _____

   *Have you talked to your future spouse about those decisions so that you can begin to come to unity before you get married? _____

Unifying Differences

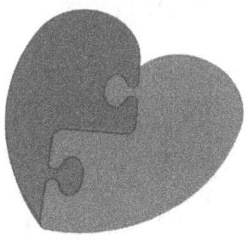

A perfect picture is formed
by joining many different parts in perfect harmony

Genesis 2:24b
... __THEY__ shall be __ONE__ flesh.

l + 1 = 1

Mark 10:8-9
*And they __TWAIN__ shall be __ONE__ flesh:
so then they are no more __TWAIN__, but __ONE__ flesh.
What therefore God hath __JOINED__ together,
let not man put __ASUNDER__.*

Ephesians 5:31b
... and they __TWO__ shall be __ONE__ flesh.

The Necessity of Humility for True Unity
From the life of Ruth and Boaz in the Book of Ruth

Proverbs 13:10a
Only by PRIDE cometh contention:

Ruth	Boaz
Culture	
From Moab (1:4, 2:1, 10-13)	From Isreal (2:1)
Family	
Widow (1:3-5)	Single (4:6)
Finances	
Poor (beggar) (2:2, 7)	Rich (2:1)
Job	
Lowly worker (2:7)	Business owner (2:8)
Age	
Young (2:5, 4:10b)	Old (2:8a, 3:10-11)

Proverbs 29:23
A man's pride shall bring him low:
But honour shall uphold the humble in spirit.

Ruth	Boaz
Served Naomí (1:16-17, 2:11)	Served Ruth (2:14-16)
Honored Boas (2:10)	Saught to do what was just (3:12-13)
Depended in God (2:12)	Protected and provided for Ruth (3:14-15)
Obeyed Naomi's councel (3:1-6)	Asked permission to marry Ruth (4:1-10)
Asked for Boaz's help (3:9)	

Proverbs 16:19
Better it is to be of an humble spirit with the lowly,
Than to divide the spoil with the proud.

Proverbs 22:4
By humility and the fear of the LORD
are riches, and honour, and life.

Ruth and Boaz enjoyed <u>riches</u> together (4:10-12)

Ruth and Boaz received <u>honor</u> together (4:13, 15)

Ruth and Boaz produced <u>life</u> together (4:13b-14, 17)

I Peter 5:5-7
... Yea, all of you be subject one to another,
and be clothed with humility:
for God resisteth the proud,
and giveth grace to the humble.
Humble yourselves therefore
under the mighty hand of God,
that he may exalt you in due time:
Casting all your care upon him;
for he careth for you.

Chapter 4

Article IV
The Roles in the Marriage Covenant
Genesis 2:16-20

Adam and Eve were created to be two different sides of the same coin. God's design is that a man and a woman be permanently joined together to form one entity while each individual fulfills their created role. Before woman was created, God said that man's condition was not *"good"* because he was *"alone"* (Genesis 2:18). And without man, woman's created purpose of being a *"help meet"* could not have been fulfilled (Genesis 2:18).

The Roles of the Man and Woman

The Role of the Man as Leader

Before Eve was created by God for Adam, God gave Adam a decision-making and leadership task to accomplish. Genesis 2:19-20 say, ***"And out of the ground the LORD God formed every beast of the field, and every fowl of the air; and brought them unto Adam to see what he would call them: and whatsoever Adam called every living creature, that was the name thereof. And Adam gave names to all cattle, and to the fowl of the air, and to every beast of the field ..."*** Adam's first task was to name each and every animal. He had the choice and the authority to give each the name by which they would be known for the rest of time. Man, in his perfect state, was created to receive instruction, make choices, and then be a leader in carrying out the decisions made.

❤The Roles in the Marriage Covenant ❤

The Role of the Woman as Helper

When Adam was finished naming the animals the Bible says, *"but for Adam there was not found an help meet for him."* (Genesis 2:20). Adam's *"help meet"* was not found among the animals, but rather God took action in verses 21 and 22 to create Eve directly from Adam as an equal to Adam. As God created Eve, He did so with one key role or attribute in His design. Genesis 2:18 provides God's design for Adam's wife in God's own words as He said, *"I will make him an help meet for him."* God's designed role for woman is that of a helper. Adam was created first and therefore given the leadership role (I Timothy 2:12-13). Eve was created second in order to assist Adam in his life and tasks. Adam did not need a maid, cook, mother, or lover. He needed an assistant perfectly created to fill in the voids of his life. Proverbs 18:22 says, *"Whoso findeth a wife findeth a good thing, and obtaineth favour of the LORD."* Therefore, a woman is not any less important than the man, because God said that man was not good or complete without her. But she is to accomplish the purpose for which she was designed: to complete her husband's life. Woman, in her perfect state was created to assist man in the tasks God gave them.

❤ *Are we ready to accept our personal roles specified in the Marriage Covenant?*

The Danger of Role Failure Between a Husband and Wife

God's instruction for Adam and Eve's spiritual well-being extended into their roles. Genesis 2:16-17 says, *"And the LORD God commanded the man, saying, Of every tree of the garden thou mayest freely eat: but of the tree of the knowledge of good and evil, thou shalt not eat of it: for in the day that thou eatest thereof thou shalt surely die.*" God gave Adam His message before Eve was created. Then in Genesis 3:2-3 we find Eve presenting this same instruction to Satan. Based on I Corinthians 14:34-35 which says, *"... and if they [women] will learn any thing, let them ask their husbands at home ...,"* it is safe to assume that Adam as the spiritual leader communicated to Eve God's instruction.

Next, when God came to confront the couple for hiding from Him, He addressed Adam first. Adam was given the leadership role in the relationship and now he would need to be the first one to answer for their failure (Luke 12:47-48).

Finally, as God presents Adam with his punishment for sinning, He begins with, *"Because thou hast hearkened unto the voice of thy wife ..."* (Genesis 3:17). As Adam chose to eat of the forbidden fruit his wife presented to him and encouraged him to eat, he chose to directly disobey God for the first time. As a result, it would seem that Eve's new sinful words and wishes were of more value to him than his role of leading her to do right. Later, when he was confronted by God, Adam even attempted to blame her (and God) for his sin by saying, *"The woman whom thou gavest to be with me, she gave me of the tree, and I did eat"* (Genesis 3:12).

Unfortunately, Eve, in her new sinful condition, encouraged Adam to sin with her, rather than being his spiritual helpmeet by supporting him in his obedience to God and his leadership of her to do the same, as *"... she took of the fruit thereof, and did eat, and gave also unto her husband with her; and he did eat"* (Genesis 3:6). Eve sinned and immediately she turned Adam and undermined God's commandment and her husband's leadership by offering him an opportunity to disobey the very commandment of God that he had previously shared with her. Following Eve's sin, she began to fail in her role as a proper helpmeet as she did not encourage her husband to fulfill his created purpose of obeying and glorifying God, but rather encouraged him to rebel against God by disobeying His Word.

❤ The Roles in the Marriage Covenant ❤

Later, as God presented Eve her punishment for her sin, He reiterated her role under her husband's leadership by saying, *"... and thy desire shall be to thy husband, and he shall rule over thee."* (Genesis 3:16). Do not misunderstand, God's leadership roles are established for protection and not humiliation (Numbers 30:1-16). I Timothy 2:12-14 say, *"... And Adam was not deceived, but the woman being deceived was in the transgression."* If the wife will seek the leadership protection of her husband when she is tempted, and the husband will only heed his wife words when they do not violate God's Word, many marital sins can been avoided. God established the husband's leadership role as protection for his wife, as he, the husband, obeys God's leadership and is protected by Him. For this to work, I Corinthians 11:3 must be understood and heeded as it says, *"But I would have you know, that the head of every man is Christ; and the head of the woman is the man; and the head of Christ is God."*

❤ Are we ready to accept each other in our specific roles specified in the Marriage Covenant?

The Equality of the Man and Woman

Genesis 2:18-20 says, *"And the LORD God said, It is not good that the man should be alone; I will make him an help meet for him. And out of the ground the LORD God formed every beast of the field, and every fowl of the air; and brought them unto Adam to see what he would call them: and whatsoever Adam called every living creature, that was the name thereof. And Adam gave names to all cattle, and to the fowl of the air, and to every beast of the field; but for Adam there was not found an help meet for him."* God, in His wisdom, knew that man needed a companion and helper (Genesis 2:18). Instead of creating a woman immediately, He created and brought before man all the animals of the world. It is very possible that as he looked at every new animal, he was actually looking for the *"help meet"* God said he needed. However, *"but for Adam there was not found a help meet for him"* (Genesis 2:20b). No animal would do. Adam needed a helper who was *"meet for him,"* or adequate for and equal to him. He needed a helper made from his side, to stand by his side. Woman was the perfect creation, equal to Adam and prepared for the task of being his helper.

The world today calls for equality of men and women. God does not deny equality, He simply specifies their roles.

Equality Based on Physical Life

The man and woman are equally important and necessary in the process of producing life. I Corinthians 11:11-12 says, *"Nevertheless neither is the man without the woman, neither the woman without the man, in the Lord. For as the woman is of the man, even so is the man also by the woman; but all things of God."* Both man and woman are dependent on each other for life and fulfilment. Without man, woman would not exist (Genesis 2:21-23), and without woman, man ceases to be. Both man and woman are equally important in the completion of God's command to *"Be fruitful, and multiply, and replenish the earth, and subdue it ..."* (Genesis 1:28).

I Corinthians 7:4 teaches the equality of the husband and wife as it gives the authority over their bodies to the other individual when it says, *"The wife hath not power of her own body, but the husband: and likewise also the husband hath not power of his own body, but the wife."* And verses 33-34 add to the equality of the husband and wife as they say, *"But he that is married careth for ... how he may please his wife ... she that is married careth for ... how she may please her husband."* A husband and wife are equally responsible to dedicate their bodies and lives to each other's wishes and needs. They are to equally seek to please the other so as to build their relationship by displaying biblical love.

Equality Based on Spiritual Life

God is very clear that each individual is significant to Him (Romans 2:11, Colossians 3:11). This spiritual significance and equality is also seen between a husband and wife as Peter provides instruction to the husband and says, ***"Likewise, ye husbands, dwell with them according to knowledge, giving honour unto the wife, as unto the weaker vessel, and as being heirs together of the grace of life; that your prayers be not hindered"*** (I Peter 3:7). The spiritual equality of the woman is not only presented, but the man is given a warning that if he does not treat her correctly, his spiritual condition will be affected. Each individual is equally important and of equal value (Luke 12:6-7).

❤ *Do we accept each other's value and equality before God?*

❧Relationship Building Questions❧
Article IV

1. What are the God-given roles for the man and woman?
   a. Man: _____
      (Genesis 2:19-20, I Timothy 2:12-13)
   b. Woman: _____
      (Genesis 2:18-20)
   How can a husband show loving leadership to his wife?
      i. _____
      ii. _____
      iii. _____
   How can a wife show humble submission to her husband?
      i. _____
      ii. _____
      iii. _____

2. What is the leadership order in a Christian marriage (I Corinthians 11:3)?
   a. _____
   b. _____
   c. _____
   d. _____
   Who should provide human spiritual leadership and guidance in the marriage? (I Corinthians 14:34-35) _____

   How can a husband be prepared to give his wife the spiritual leadership she needs? _____
   _____
   _____

♥The Roles in the Marriage Covenant ♥

3. What is the result of "role failure" in the marriage covenant?
   _____
   _____

   What are some ways which "role failure" could be displayed in relationships today?
   a. _____
   b. _____
   c. _____

4. In what two ways does the Bible express the equality of a man and woman?
   a. I Corinthians 11:11-12 _____
   b. I Peter 3:7 _____

Recognizing the Differences Between Men and Women
Genesis 1-3

Genesis 1:26-31
Joint creation with equal value and unified purpose.
Value - In the image of God
(Spiritual - I Peter 3:7)
Purpose - Reproduction & Global Dominion
(Physical - I Corinthians 11:11-12)

Genesis 2:7-25
Separate creation with particular roles.
(I Timothy 2:12-14)

Men	Women
Leader (7, 16-17, 23-24)	Companion (18)
Worker (15)	Helper (18, 20)
Decision Maker (19-20, 23)	Dependent (23)
Note - Adam rested before he met Eve (21)	*Note - Adam named woman based on his name, "man," and then changed it to Eve (23, 20)*

*What God has established by perfect creation, the flesh, the world, and the Devil will try to distort and reverse.

Genesis 3:1-6 Inception of sin brought about in different ways. *(I Timothy 2:14)*	
Men	**Women**
Chooser (6)	Deceivable (1-6) (Questioner, Detailer)
Genesis 3:7–8 Result of sin is shame and cover-up for both.	
Genesis 3:9 God's call to the man to confront the situation.	
Genesis 3:9-13 Confrontation for sin provides God's view and man & woman's flesh.	
Men	**Women**
First - Primary Responsibility (9, 12) Blame shifter (12)	Second - Secondary Responsibility (13) Blame shifter (13)
Genesis 3:16-25 Separate judgement reveals particular roles and responsibilities.	
Men	**Women**
Leader (17a) Worker (17b-19a)	Subject (16b) Mother (16a)

A Practical Understanding of Men & Women
Based On Adam and Eve

*When we consider how and why God created man and woman in Genesis 2:7-25, we can understand why we are so different and why we think, feel, and act so differently in any given situation. These differences are not meant to destroy us, but rather to complete us. A "well rounded" Christian couple will embrace each other's differences as God's personal assistance through each other's lives. They will be able to answer the fundamental question of why does he/she think, act, say, etc., so that they can build each other up rather than tear each other down. Here are a few general categories in which men and women are frequently differ.

Men	**Women**
Leader	**Companion**
(7, 16-17, 23-24)	**(18)**
1. Seeks respect	1. Seeks love
2. Interested in doing	2. Interested in being
3. More competition oriented	3. More personal oriented
4. Goals oriented	4. Social oriented
5. Decisions based on knowledge	5. Decisions based on emotions
6. Stimulated by sight	6. Stimulated by touch

*Adapted from materials presented in the Christian Family class, Dr. Wynne Kimbrough, NBBC, 1996, page 20. Used by Permission.

Worker (15)	**Helper** (18, 20)
7. Vocation oriented	7. Relationship oriented
8. Find fulfillment in work	8. Find fulfillment in home and children
9. Logic based	9. Intuition based
10. Awareness of responsibilities	10. Awareness of presence
11. Big picture	11. Small details
12. Achievers (business)	12. Care taker (home)
13. Physically violent	13. Verbally violent
14. "Compartmentalized" thinking	14. "Multi-tasker/thinker"
15. Concerned with externals	15. Concerned with internals
16. Investment in things	16. Investment in people
17. More earthly minded	17. More spiritually minded

Decision Maker (19-20, 23)	**Dependent** (23)
18. Quality time to consider options	18. Quality time to be heard and understood
19. Speak from head	19. Speak from heart
20. Self assurance	20. Needs reassurance
21. Take chances	21. Want security
22. Insensitive	22. Vulnerable and sensitive

*Adapted from materials presented in the Christian Family class, Dr. Wynne Kimbrough, NBBC, 1996, page 20. Used by Permission.

Admirable Characteristics for a Life-Long Relationship as Displayed by Boaz and Ruth
Ruth 1-4

9 Admirable Characteristics for the Husband

1. **Leadership** (2:1, 4) - A husband should provide leadership for his wife in both the spiritual and everyday decisions.
2. **Attentiveness** (2:5, 7, 11, 3:8-10) - A husband should pay attention to and complementary of his wife's appearance and actions.
3. **Provider** (2:8-9, 14-16, 3:15) - A husband should seek to provide for his wife's needs.
4. **Protector** (2:9-16, 3:14) - A husband should be aware of the dangers surrounding his wife and offer his protection.
5. **Kindness** (2:13-14) - A husband should show kindness to his wife with his words and actions.
6. **Humility** (3:10) - A husband must be humble and appreciative that his wife has chosen him to be her husband.
7. **Honor** (3:11-13, 18) - A husband must treat his wife with honor and reassure her that he will do his part to resolve any difficulties they encounter.
8. **Integrity** (4:1-12) - A husband must always fulfill his responsibilities with his wife and others with the utmost integrity both in public and private.
9. **Sharing** (4:10, 13) - A husband must share his home, life, and himself with his wife.

9 Admirable Characteristics for the Wife

1. **Commitment** (1:14-22, 2:6-7, 3:5, 11) - A wife should be committed to follow her husband's leadership both in the spiritual and day-to-day decisions.
2. **Diligence** (2:2-3, 7) - A wife should be diligent in her work and fulfilling her part of providing for her family.
3. **Respectfulness** (2:7, 10) - A wife should be respectful in her speech by entreating him and showing respect with her words and actions.
4. **Appreciation** (2:10, 13) - A wife should display appreciation for the provision and protection of her husband.
5. **Trust** (2:12-13) - A wife should trust both God and her husband to provide, protect, and guide her life.
6. **Receptiveness** (3:1-8) - A wife should be willing to receive and follow godly counsel about her relationship with her husband.
7. **Patience** (3:18) - A wife should patiently wait for her husband's decisions and the time it take for him to fulfill his commitments.
8. **Virtue** (3:11) - A wife should maintain a virtuous testimony in public and in private.
9. **Sharing** (4:10, 13) - A wife should share her home, life, and herself with her husband.

Chapter 5

Article V
The Responsibilities of the Marriage Covenant
Genesis 1:27-31, 3:16-17

The Joint Responsibilities of Man and Woman

In Genesis 1:27-31 God gave man and woman their general responsibilities when he said, *"So God created man in his own image, in the image of God created he him; male and female created he them. And God blessed them, and God said unto them, Be fruitful, and multiply, and replenish the earth, and subdue it: and have dominion over the fish of the sea, and over the fowl of the air, and over every living thing that moveth upon the earth. And God said, Behold, I have given you every herb bearing seed, which is upon the face of all the earth, and every tree, in the which is the fruit of a tree yielding seed; to you it shall be for meat. And to every beast of the earth, and to every fowl of the air, and to every thing that creepeth upon the earth, wherein there is life, I have given every green herb for meat: and it was so. And God saw every thing that he had made, and, behold, it was very good. And the evening and the morning were the sixth day."*

On the sixth day of creation God perfectly created both man and woman to fulfill specific roles so that they could accomplish the responsibility of all mankind. They were to begin a family and take charge of the newly created world. The husband was to fulfill his role by leading while his wife was to fulfill her role by assisting her husband in every task they encountered.

❤ *Are we looking forward to working together as we fulfill our God-given responsibilities?*

❤The Responsibilities of the Marriage Covenant❤

The Individual Responsibility of Man and Woman

God's presentation of Adam and Eve's punishment provides more insight as to the individual roles He desires for a husband and wife. In Genesis 3:16-17 God tells Eve, *"Unto the woman he said, I will greatly multiply thy sorrow and thy conception; in sorrow thou shalt bring forth children; and thy desire shall be to thy husband, and he shall rule over thee. And unto Adam he said, Because thou hast hearkened unto the voice of thy wife, and hast eaten of the tree, of which I commanded thee, saying, Thou shalt not eat of it: ..."* God made it very clear that the husband was to be the leader and the woman was to follow. Therefore, the responsibilities of the man and woman would fit their specific roles.

Ephesians 5:22-33 helps to explain more fully the way in which the husband and wife are to work together in their particular roles to fulfill their overall responsibility given in Genesis 1:27-31. In this passage both the husband's and wife's private responsibilities are compared to the relationship of Jesus Christ and the church. Let's consider the teaching of this passage as well as other similar passages throughout the New Testament to help us find the specific responsibilities given to each member of the marriage team.

*The husband's responsibilities
are founded in loving leadership*

Ephesians 5:25-32 says, *"Husbands, love your wives, even as Christ also loved the church, and gave himself for it; that he might sanctify and cleanse it with the washing of water by the word, that he might present it to himself a glorious church, not having spot, or wrinkle, or any such thing; but that it should be holy and without blemish. So ought men to love their wives as their own bodies. He that loveth his wife loveth himself. For no man ever yet hated his own flesh; but nourisheth and cherisheth it, even as the Lord the church: For we are members of his body, of his flesh, and of his bones. For this cause shall a man leave his father and mother, and shall be joined unto his wife, and they two shall be one flesh. This is a great mystery: but I speak concerning Christ and the church.*" The husband's responsibility is to represent Jesus Christ to his wife, not in his own power or authority, but by the loving power and authority of God. The husband must recognize the significant responsibility he has and fulfill it with the utmost care. His leadership is not a dictatorship, but a presence of direction and protection. He must be a leader who is willing to sacrifice every position, right, and power in love for the good of his wife. Jesus Christ provides an example of proper loving leadership as he "*... being in the form of God, thought it not robbery to be equal with God: but made himself of no reputation, and took upon him the form of a servant, and was made in the likeness of men: and being found in fashion as a man, he humbled himself, and became obedient unto death, even the death of the cross*" (Philippians 2:6-8). A husband must lovingly care for his wife as he does for himself because "*... he that loveth his wife loveth himself. For no man ever yet hated his own flesh; but nourisheth and cherisheth it, even as the Lord the church*" (Ephesians 5:28-29).

- ♦ He is to love his wife with a sacrificial love (25, 28-29).

    *Colossians 3:19

    *I Peter 3:7

- ♦ He is to be a spiritual leader by guiding his wife with the Word of God so that she might be without spiritual blemish (26).

    *I Corinthians 14:34-35

- ♦ He is to care for and protect his wife (29).

    *I Timothy 5:8

Loving leadership is prepared and protective leadership. A husband who is fulling his responsibilities as a leader will constantly be growing spiritually so that he can provide guidance

♥The Responsibilities of the Marriage Covenant♥

for his wife as she has questions and concerns (I Corinthians 14:34-35). He will also be alert to the current and future attacks which his family is facing so that he can properly protect them from destruction. Proverbs 22:3 says, *"A prudent man foreseeth the evil, and hideth himself: but the simple pass on, and are punished."*

The husband's leadership can be likened to the lead car in a caravan, on a dark night, and on windy roads. The lead car's headlights not only provide illumination for itself, but also extend the illumination for the cars which follow. And, as the lead driver makes wise decisions, he helps provide the other drivers with clear direction for each of their decisions. However, as the lights dim and decisions falter, the lead car and driver begin to loose their helpfulness and can actually lead other cars into grave danger. For this reason, a Christian husband must be daily in the Word of God so that it can be *"a lamp unto my [his] feet, and a light unto my [his] path"* (Psalm 1119:105). He must look to God for each decision and depend upon His promise of, *"I will instruct thee and teach thee in the way which thou shalt go: I will guide thee with mine eye"* (Psalm 32:8).

♥ *As a husband, am I prepared to lovingly lead my wife no matter what the sacrifice to my personal well-being or desires?*

♥The Responsibilities of the Marriage Covenant♥

Husband's Responsibilities to His Wife

Ephesians 5:25-33
  Love (like Christ)
  Nourish & Cherish (like his own body)
  Love (as himself)
Colossians 3:19
  Love
  Not bitter (not produce a bitter taste in their mouth)
I Timothy 5:8
  Provide (attend to the needs of)
I Peter 3:7
  Dwell (be with)
  Know (to study, learn and apply)
  Honour (as a weaker vessel & fellow believer)

A Husband's Example of Fulfilled Responsibilities
Joseph & Mary
Matthew 1:18-25, 2:13-15

1. Love - He did not desire to make her a public example (18-19)
2. Love, Nourish, Not Bitter, Provide, Dwell, Know - He did not put her away privately, but in obedience, brought her into his own home (he could have been greatly shamed for this) (20-24)
3. Honour - He did not "know" his wife, but honored her virgin pregnancy (25)

♥The Responsibilities of the Marriage Covenant♥

The wife's responsibilities are found in a submissive helpfulness

Ephesians 5:22-24 and 33 say, *"Wives, submit yourselves unto your own husbands, as unto the Lord. For the husband is the head of the wife, even as Christ is the head of the church: and he is the saviour of the body. Therefore as the church is subject unto Christ, so let the wives be to their own husbands in every thing"* and *"... see that she reverence her husband."* The wife's responsibility is to be submissive to the leadership of her husband. Submission is not passivism or slavery. It is a personal choice to relinquish personal positions, rights, and power to the leadership of another. Jesus Christ provides the perfect example of submissive obedience with his death on the cross. In John 10:17-18 Jesus said, *"Therefore doth my Father love me, because I lay down my life, that I might take it again. No man taketh it from me, but I lay it down of myself. I have power to lay it down, and I have power to take it again. This commandment have I received of my Father."* A wife should not be forced by human means to honor the leadership of her husband. She should follow the example of the Church's submissive obedience to Jesus Christ, *"Jesus Christ is the head of the body, the church ..."* (Colossians 1:18), which is to say that He is the decision maker. Where the head leads, the body naturally follows. So should a wife willingly and readily submit herself to God's authority over the home by following the leadership of her husband.

- ♦ She is to be submissive (subject) to her husband (22-24).
- ♦ As she is submissive to the Lord (based on the Lord's authority) (22).

  *Colossians 3:18
- ♦ Based on the example of the church's responsibility to follow Jesus Christ (23-24).
- ♦ In every area of her life and their relationship (24b).

♥The Responsibilities of the Marriage Covenant♥

♦ She is to reverence (honor) her husband (33).

Submissive helpfulness is meek supportiveness. A wife who is fulfilling her responsibility will follow God's instruction to *"be in subjection to your own husbands"* with *"a meek and quiet spirit, which is in the sight of God of great price"* (I Peter 3:1-4). She will seek to wisely make choices which will be a blessing to her husband and family. Proverbs 19:14 says, *"House and riches are the inheritance of fathers: and a prudent wife is from the LORD."*

A wife's submissive helpfulness can be likened to a good seasoning for a meal. When there is not enough seasoning, the food is bland. When there is too much seasoning, the food is over-powering. However when the seasoning is just right, it fully enhances the food's original flavors, and in turn receives it's proper praise. Likewise, when a wife properly seasons her husband's life with her helpful wisdom and abilities, she assists in producing a relationship which is very savory for the world around them to enjoy and in turn she receives high praise (Psalm 31:10-31).

♥ *As a wife, am I prepared to humbly follow the leadership of my husband no matter what the sacrifice to my personal well-being or desires?*

❤The Responsibilities of the Marriage Covenant❤

Wife's Responsibilities to Her Husband

Ephesians 5:22-23, 33
    Submit (as unto the Lord)
    Be subject (like the church is to Christ)
    Reverence
Colossians 3:18
    Submit (as it is fit in the Lord)
Titus 2:1, 3-5
    Love her husband
    Love her children (her husband's children)
    Keeper at home (her husband's home)
    Obedient (to her husband)
I Peter 3:1-6
    Be subject
    Be a sight (of chaste conversation with fear)
        Adorned (meekness & quietness)

A Wife's Example of Fulfilled Responsibilities
Proverbs 31:10-31

1. Reverence - Her husband has more honor because of her testimony (11-12, 23)
2. Submit, Subject - Her work displays her helpfulness and dedication (13-21, 24, 27)
3. Reverence - Her speech displays respect in wisdom and kindness
4. Be a sight, Adorned - Her beauty is much deeper than her outward appearance (30)

❧Relationship Building Questions❧
Article V

1. What are the two responsibilities given to Adam and Eve?
   a. _____
   b. _____
   What family tasks will you need to work on together to accomplish based upon your individual responsibilities?
   a. _____
   b. _____
   c. _____
   d. _____
   e. _____

2. What are the God-given responsibilities of a husband? (Ephesians 5:25-33, Colossians 3:19, I Timothy 5:8, I Peter 3:7)
   a. _____
   b. _____
   c. _____
   d. _____
   e. _____
   f. _____
   g. _____

3. How can a husband practically fulfill his responsibility of leading his wife in love?
   a. _____
   b. _____
   c. _____
   d. _____
   How can a husband prepare himself to be a spiritual leader?
   _____
   _____

♥The Responsibilities of the Marriage Covenant♥

4. What are the God-given responsibilities of a wife? (Ephesians 5:22-33, Colossians 3:18, Titus 2:1, 3-5, I Peter 3:1-6)
   a. _____
   b. _____
   c. _____
   d. _____
   e. _____
   f. _____
   g. _____

5. How can a wife practically fulfill her responsibility of being a helper to her husband while submitting to his leadership?
   a. _____
   b. _____
   c. _____
   d. _____

   How can a wife encourage her husband to be the spiritual leader? _____
   _____
   _____

♥The Responsibilities of the Marriage Covenant♥

6. Groom - Based on Ephesians 5:33 and I Peter 2:7, what are three new things you have learned about your bride and how can you display your love to her based on this knowledge?
   a. _____
   b. _____
   c. _____
   *How can you love her even when she fails you?
   _____
   _____
   _____

   Bride - Based on Ephesians 5:33, what are three things about your groom with which you can honor him?
   a. _____
   b. _____
   c. _____
   *How can you honor him even when he fails you?
   _____
   _____
   _____

Reality of Responsibility

God has provided the husband and wife with very specific responsibilities. Take some time to describe how an obedient husband and wife may practically fulfill these responsibilities on a daily basis.

Husband's Responsibilities to His Wife

The Spiritual Husband	The Practical Husband
Ephesians 5:25-33	
Love (like Christ)	
Nourish & Cherish (like his own body)	
Love (as himself)	
Colossians 3:19	
Love	
Not bitter (not produce a bitter taste in the mouth)	
I Timothy 5:8	
Provide (attend to the needs of)	
I Peter 3:7	
Dwell (be with)	
Know (to study, learn and apply)	
Honor (as a weaker vessel & fellow believer)	

Wife's Responsibilities to Her Husband

The Spiritual Wife	The Practical Wife
Ephesians 5:22-33	
Submit (as unto the Lord)	
Be subject (like the church is to Christ)	
Reverence	
Colossians 3:18	
Submit (as it is fit in the Lord)	
I Peter 3:16	
Be subject	
Be a sight (of chaste conversation)	
Adorned (meekness & quietness)	

Reversal of Responsibility

Satan, the World, and the Flesh always attempt to reverse or distort what God has perfectly made. The same is true for the responsibilities given to the husband and wife. Take some time to describe what each of these responsibilities would look like if they were reversed.

Husband's Responsibilities to His Wife

The Spiritual Husband	The Practical Husband
Ephesians 5:25-33	
Love (like Christ)	
Nourish & Cherish (like his own body)	
Love (as himself)	
Colossians 3:19	
Love	
Not bitter (not produce a bitter taste in the mouth)	
I Timothy 5:8	
Provide (attend to the needs of)	
I Peter 3:7	
Dwell (be with)	
Know (to study, learn and apply)	
Honor (as a weaker vessel & fellow believer)	

Wife's Responsibilities to Her Husband

The Spiritual Wife	The Fleshly Wife
Ephesians 5:22-33	
Submit (as unto the Lord)	
Be subject (like the church is to Christ)	
Reverence	
Colossians 3:18	
Submit (as it is fit in the Lord)	
I Peter 3:16	
Be subject	
Be a sight (of chaste conversation)	
Adorned (meekness & quietness)	

Chapter 6

Article VI
The Terms of the Marriage Covenant
Genesis 2:24, 3:7-8

A Marriage Covenant is best signed by two best friends. Genesis 2:24 says that the man *"shall cleave unto his wife: and they shall be one flesh."* A proper Christian marriage is made up of a man and woman who are "glued" together. They spend time together, share life experiences together, and enjoy communicating together. The same is true for friendship. Proverbs 18:24 says, *"... there is a friend that sticketh closer than a brother."* What better place to find a friendship in which two individuals are "glued" or "cleaving" together than the one flesh relationship in marriage. In the marriage relationship the husband and wife should be such friends that their own blood relationships cannot be compared to their closeness together. (ie. Mother, father, brother–Genesis 2:24, Proverbs 18:24). However, Proverbs 18:24 begins with an important principle.

Before two individuals can be close friends they must *"shew himself [themselves] friendly."* Throughout time, friendships have spanned the gulfs of distance, culture, background, status, age, etc. with the bridge of constant and honest communication (I Samuel 18:1-4). Communication reveals a dedication to the relationship and fulfills the standard that *"a friend loveth at all times ..."* (Proverbs 17:17). Communication is the key to being married to your BEST friend. The Marriage Covenant is best fulfilled when two friends are walking hand in hand sharing life's experiences, and communicating their personal thoughts, feelings, plans, etc., along the way.

❤ *Are we ready to make each other our BEST friend for life?*

❤The Terms of the Marriage Covenant❤

Communication About the Past

In any written Covenant, small print is not appreciated. The same is true for a working marriage. "Small print" before or during marriage always reveals secrets and the possibility for shame due to sin being covered up. In Genesis 3:7-8 we find that after Adam and Eve sinned *"... the eyes of them both were opened, and they knew that they were naked; and they sewed fig leaves together, and made themselves aprons. And they heard the voice of the LORD God walking in the garden in the cool of the day: and Adam and his wife hid themselves from the presence of the LORD God amongst the trees of the garden."*

Adam and Eve's first response after realizing their sin was to cover themselves from each other. They also attempted to hide themselves from God. For the first time in their relationship there was SHAME. When there has been sin in the past which has not been confessed and forsaken biblically, guilt remains. Personal guilt can be covered from man for a time, but God will always bring it to the surface so that it can be dealt with correctly. Proverbs 28:13 says, *"He that covereth his sins shall not prosper: but whoso confesseth and forsaketh them shall have mercy."*

When there has been sin in our past which has been confessed and forsaken Biblically, I John 1:9 promises, *"If we confess our sins, he is faithful and just to forgive us our sins, and to cleanse us from all unrighteousness."* There is no reason for guilt to linger longer (Romans 8:33-34, I John 3:19-22), although shame or proper sorrow about the sin and the affects of that sin may still remain. The end result of Adam and Eve's sin followed them through the rest of their lives. The same is true for the husband-wife relationship today. Galatians 6:7-8 present the simple principle of sowing and reaping when it says, *"Be not deceived; God is not mocked: for whatsoever a man soweth, that shall he also reap. For he that soweth to his flesh shall of the flesh reap*

♥The Terms of the Marriage Covenant♥

corruption; but he that soweth to the Spirit shall of the Spirit reap life everlasting."

Before and throughout the marriage relationship it is of the utmost importance that both individuals are "painfully" honest with each other about any area of their lives in which they have sowed to the flesh and now may reap the fruit of that sin in their relationship. To use the words of Scripture, they must tell the "naked" truth so that there are no "aprons" to cover up small print which will be revealed years later (Genesis 2:25, 3:7). This process is not easy, nor is it necessary in every dating relationship. However, as the Marriage Covenant is being considered, there must be no secrets. This is not to indicate that every detail must be revealed, but the general subjects, sins, and incidences must be addressed adequately and any questions or concerns must be answered (even to the extent of further biblical counsel being provided) so that there is total openness and perfect unity when the Marriage Covenant is signed.

Please do not be fooled by Satan's lie that "it really does not matter, the past is the past." It does matter! Every thing that has taken place in your past has made you who you are today, and therefore will go with you into your marriage, whether good or bad. The good will provide joy and is easy to share with your partner, but the bad will bring shame and brings the risk of doing great damage to your Marriage Covenant if not dealt with honestly and correctly before hand.

♥ *Have we been totally honest with each other about our past lives and relationships?*

♥ *Do we have any questions that have not been answered adequately about each other's past?*

♥The Terms of the Marriage Covenant♥

Communication For the Future

During a marital relationship, "small print" must be avoided at all cost. The old adage "what he/she doesn't know won't hurt him/her" really is NOT true! *"For there is nothing covered, that shall not be revealed; neither hid, that shall not be known"* (Luke 12:2). Proper communication and honesty are needed to bring a couple to the point of signing the Marriage Covenant and it is the only way that the Marriage Covenant can be fulfilled correctly. Genesis 2:24 says that a husband and wife are *"one flesh."* The one flesh relationship demands proper and regular communication to stay healthy. A physical body is a great illustration of the marriage relationship. Our bodies are full of communication pathways and receptacles called the Nervous System. The Nervous System communicates instinctively and almost immediately throughout the entire body both internally and externally. It communicates sensations of pain, pleasure, etc. When an area of the body does not communicate correctly it is said to be "numb." When any area of the body goes numb, there are immediate health concerns. If the numbness continues for a length of time, that area of the body can be seriously damaged (i.e. cut, burned, bruised) without the rest of the body knowing to take care of its needs or help solve its problems. The same is true in the one flesh relationship in marriage. When communication is broken, a problem is revealed that must be dealt with as quickly as possible so that long term numbness and further damage does not set in.

For the marriage relationship to thrive there must be constant and open communication at all times. However, when numbness has been encountered, the "waking up" of the numb area of the physical body may be awkward or even painful and must be handled with care. In like manner, the process of solving the numbness of communication in the marriage relationship should be handled with loving patience until full restoration and resolution has been accomplished (Galatians 6:1-2, James

5:19-20). Proper communication must be reestablished with loving care. There must be removal of all *"... **anger, wrath, malice, blasphemy, filthy communication out of your mouth. Lie not one to another ...**"* (Colossians 3:8-9a). The foundational rule for all communication should be **"*Let your speech be alway with grace, seasoned with salt, that ye may know how ye ought to answer every man*"** (Colossians 4:6). Ephesians 4:29 explains this rule a little more by saying, **"*Let no corrupt communication proceed out of your mouth, but that which is good to the use of edifying, that it may minister grace unto the hearers.*"**

❤ *Are we practicing proper communication now by sharing our thoughts, plans, and feelings openly with each other?*

❤ *Are we working through our present areas of disagreement by properly communicating with each other until a unified decision is reached?*

❤ *Are we committed to communicate regularly and honestly about every aspect of our lives as we enjoy our "one flesh" or permanently unified relationship?*

*For further biblical instruction about communication, consider the teaching of the book of Proverbs as well as James 3:1-12.

❧Relationship Building Questions❧
Article V

1. How are we growing in our knowledge of and friendship with each other?
   a. _____
   b. _____
   c. _____

2. Who is our best friend (of the same gender)?
   a. Man: _____
   b. Woman: _____
   Are we willing to give up these friendships in order to make each other our best friends? _____

3. Have we been open and honest about:
   ❏ Family
   ❏ Past relationships
   ❏ Extraordinary life circumstances
   ❏ Life affecting sins
   ❏ Finances
   ❏ Health
   ❏ Personal dreams

4. Have we sought forgiveness from God and others for any past life affecting sins? _____
   Have we accepted God's forgiveness for any life changing sins? (Are there any areas of our lives where there is lingering guilt?) _____

5. What are some ways that the sowing of sin in the past may affect a marriage in the future? (These ways do not need to be specific to any sins you have committed, but rather some examples.)
   a. _____
   b. _____
   c. _____

❤The Terms of the Marriage Covenant❤

6. What plans and dreams for the future have we already communicated about?
   a. _____
   b. _____
   c. _____
   d. _____
   e. _____

   What plans and dreams for the future do we still need to communicate about so that we can start to resolve any differences that may occur?
   a. _____
   b. _____
   c. _____
   d. _____
   e. _____

7. What are some ways in which we should communicate together?
   a. _____
   b. _____
   c. _____
   d. _____
   e. _____

   What are some ways in which we should not communicate together?
   a. _____
   b. _____
   c. _____
   d. _____
   e. _____

5 Levels of Communication

God's plan is for total INTIMACY in marriage
Genesis 2:25

"I AM"
Openness & Honesty
Intimacy--Total Vulnerability
Ruth 3:9-14, 4:13

"I FEEL"
Emotion
Friendship--Growing Vulnerability
Ruth 2:10, 13-14

"I THINK"
Ideas & Judgements
Co-workers--Reserved Vulnerability
Ruth 2:8-9

"I KNOW"
Facts
Familiarity--Limited Vulnerability
Ruth 2:7, 10-11

"I DO"
Cliché
Acquaintances--No Vulnerability
Ruth 2:3-5

*A Christian couple should strive to communicate on every level in order to maintain the highest level of intimacy.
*An attentive couple will recognize when a problem has caused them to stop being vulnerable with each other and thereby eliminated some levels of communication.

*Adapted from materials presented in the Christian Family class, Dr. Wynne Kimbrough, NBBC, 1996, page 33. Used by permission.

Biblical Pointers for Proper Communication

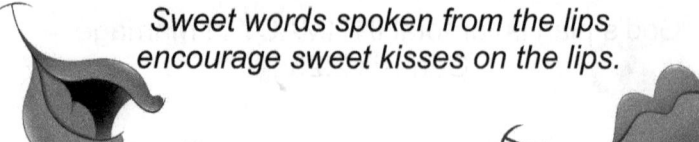

Sweet words spoken from the lips encourage sweet kisses on the lips.

- The truth can hurt, share it in love. - Ephesians 4:15, 25, Colossians 3:9
- Remember you have two ears to listen twice as much as you speak. - Proverbs 18:13, James 1:13-19
- As water quenches fire so a soft word quenches a fight - Proverbs 15:1, 25:15, 29:11
- The "silent treatment" is not treatment, it is neglect. - Ephesians 4:15, 26
- When there is nothing good to say, say nothing (But always communicate your desire to speak as soon as personal consideration and calmness are achieved). - Proverbs 10:19, 15:28, 21:23, 29:20
- "Shut up" before you "blow up" (Anger, like explosions, only destroys what it touches. But foam, like a soft tone joined with kind words helps to cushion the tension and conflict.). - Proverbs 15:1, Ephesians 4:31-32, James 1:19-20
- Never quarrel (When quarreled at, don't respond in kind) - Proverbs 17:14, 20:3, Matthew 5:39, Luke 6:31, Romans 12:17-21, 13:13, Ephesians 4:31, I Peter 2:23, 3:8-11
- Listening is not hearing, it is understanding and considering the other individuals point of view and best interest. - Proverbs 18:15, I Corinthians 10:23-24, Ephesians 4:2, Philippians 2:1-4
- Repetition is the key to learning but nagging is the key to frustration. - Proverbs 10:19, 17:9, 20:5

For further Biblical instruction about communication, consider the teaching of the book of Proverbs as well as James 3:1-12.

Chapter 7

Article VII
The Conflict in the Marriage Covenant
Genesis 3:1-8, 12-13, 17

The Cause of Marriage Conflict

Adam and Eve did not experience any conflict in their relationship until Satan put a wedge between them through temptation and sin.

The Wedge of Temptation

The first wedge of temptation was developed when Eve was encouraged to question God, as Satan said, *"Yea, hath God said"* (Genesis 3:1). This temptation to question God's wisdom, knowledge, and love can come in many forms (i.e. difficult and unexpected circumstances), but the end result is always a lack of faith that leads to sin. For this reason, God gives us the Shield of Faith with which we are to *"quench all the fiery darts of the wicked"* (Ephesians 6:16), and the promise that *"For whatsoever is born of God overcometh the world: and this is the victory that overcometh the world, even our faith"* (I John 5:4).

A husband and wife must always depend on God's revelation of Himself to them through His written Word, the Bible. They can depend on the promise that *"Grace and peace be multiplied unto you through the knowledge of God, and of Jesus our Lord, According as his divine power hath given unto us all things that pertain unto life and godliness, through the knowledge of him that hath called us to glory and virtue: Whereby are given unto us exceeding great and precious promises: that by these ye might be partakers of the divine nature, having escaped the corruption that is in the world through lust"* (II Peter 1:2-4).

♥ Do we, as a couple and as individuals, believe that God's Word is the best and final guide for every area of life?

The second wedge of temptation was developed when Eve began to live pridefully and selfishly as *"she saw that the tree was good for food, and that it was pleasant to the eyes, and a tree to be desired to make one wise"* (Genesis 3:6). Eve depended on her human understanding of the circumstances and believed that she could personally gain something from what God had forbidden. She believed that what she wanted was what she should have. It appealed to "HER," and SHE decided to take it. This is the same pattern of which James 1:14-15 speaks of, saying, *"But every man is tempted, when he is drawn away of his own lust, and enticed. Then when lust hath conceived, it bringeth forth sin: and sin, when it is finished, bringeth forth death."*

♥ Do we, as a couple and as individuals, recognize that self interest will always lead to sin and conflict?

The third wedge of temptation was developed during Adam's fall because he had *"hearkened unto the voice of thy [his] wife"* (Genesis 3:17). As Adam took a bite of the fruit offered to him by Eve, he chose to set aside his obedience to God's Word in order to obey the wrong wishes of his wife. At that moment, he set aside his God-given leadership role of doing right and leading his wife to do the same. He neglected to follow God's program, and he removed himself from God's protection. In the end God held Adam responsible for the decisions made, and Adam was required to give an account for the sin that the couple had committed (Genesis 3:9-11).

♥The Conflict in the Marriage Covenant♥

♥ *Are we, as a couple and as individuals, committed to fulfilling our personal God-given roles and to respect the role of our spouse?*

*Husbands and wives are confronted with these same three wedges every day. Satan knows that if he can get one or both of the husband and wife to mistrust, live in pride and selfishness, or relinquish their proper role, he will be able to produce sin and begin to destroy the marriage.

The Clues of Marriage Conflict

The Conviction of shame

Genesis 3:7 says, **"And the eyes of them both were opened, and they knew that they were naked ... "** Previously the Bible clearly stated that there was no shame between Adam and Eve while being naked together. Now, because they had sin in their lives, their personal innocence was lost. They were ashamed to be totally transparent and revealed to each other.

♥ *Are we committed to living together in such a way that shame does not enter our marriage?*

The Attempt to Cover Up

Genesis 3:7 goes on to say, **"... and they sewed fig leaves together, and made themselves aprons."** Adam and Eve, now ashamed of their nakedness, chose to take matters into their own hands. They did not seek God's solution so that they might be right with God. Instead, they invented their own solution which was to cover it up based on their human understanding and strength.

❤The Conflict in the Marriage Covenant❤

❤ *Are we committed to not cover up or hide things from each other in our marriage?*

The Destructive Unity (Secretism)

Genesis 3:7 indicates that Adam and Eve were unified as a couple. The Bible says *"they"* worked together to achieve the same goal. But because they did not have godly counsel, they worked together for the wrong goal of covering up their problem. Just as Eve was driven by pride to partake of the fruit and sin, now Adam and Eve are driven by pride to try to handle their marriage difficulty internally and privately. Satan loves to tempt man and woman alike to keep "private" things private. In reality, he is tempting them to stay prideful and try to deal with their situation without godly counsel and proper help. Provers 11:2 speaks clearly, **"When pride cometh, then cometh shame: but with the lowly is wisdom."** and Proverbs 16:18 adds, **"Pride goeth before destruction, and an haughty spirit before a fall."** And Proverbs 11:14 promises, **"Where no counsel is, the people fall: but in the multitude of counsellors there is safety."** A Christian married couple who desires safety must sacrifice their pride and seek godly counsel from the godly influences and authorities God has given: parents, pastors, and other mature believers (Ephesians 4:11-16, Titus 2:1-8). They must also be wary of ungodly counsel. The world will offer counsel to any situation, but it will only lead to more destruction. Proverbs 12:5 says, **"The thoughts of the righteous are right: but the counsels of the wicked are deceit."**

❤ *Are we committed to live in humility and seek biblically-based counsel and instruction for our marriage?*

❤The Conflict in the Marriage Covenant❤

The Distancing from God

Genesis 3:8 says, *"And they heard the voice of the LORD God walking in the garden in the cool of the day: and Adam and his wife hid themselves from the presence of the LORD God amongst the trees of the garden."* A husband and wife who have lost their innocence and sought to cover it up will also find themselves farther and farther from the Lord. They will find that they shrink away from their personal daily relationship with God, be it through less time in their personal devotions, prayer, opportunities to share the gospel or edify fellow believers. They may be able to continue to fulfill their Christian "obligations" for a time, but they will know that their warmth and personal love for God has been quenched (Revelations 2:1-7).

❤ *Are we committed to encourage each other to maintain a personal, daily walk with God?*

The Shifting of Blame

Genesis 3:12-13 displays more obviously the conflict between Adam and Eve when Adam says, *"The woman ... she gave me"* and Eve followed suit with, *"The serpent..."* By these comments they revealed their self-protective pride. They were confronted with their sin, but instead of humbly confessing their personal faults, their self-preserving pride began to shift the blame. When in the flesh, a husband and wife try to blame each other for their situation, division will quickly grow. Mark 3:25 warns that if *"... a house be divided against itself, that house cannot stand."* Proverbs 13:10 says, *"Only by pride cometh contention ..."*

Adam and Eve were both to blame, and they both needed to humble themselves in order to find forgiveness and restoration (I John 1:9). A husband and wife who find themselves blaming each other for whatever situation they are going through must stop immediately, confess their personal pride and whatever sins they may have committed to God and each other, and then continue in unity with God's blessing (Genesis 3:16-21).

❤ *Are we committed to accepting the blame when we do wrong and seek forgiveness and restoration?*

The Catalyst to Marriage Conflict

Personal Differences

The primary catalyst to marriage conflict can be summed up in the word "different." Differences between a married couple are not wrong. Some have said, "If a husband and wife always agree there is no need for one of them." Genesis 2:18 is clear. God said man was missing something without a woman's presence and input. For this reason, the woman was created to be different from the man specifically so that she could fill in the areas that were lacking in the man's life. Although differences in a marriage are not wrong, they can cause contention and fighting if not handled correctly. Some interpersonal differences could be as simple as what food is cooked, how to arrange furniture, the amount of time spent together, or as large as financial decisions, physical intimacy, religious beliefs and practices, child rearing, etc. However, Proverbs 13:10 simply states, **"Only by pride cometh contention: but with the well advised is wisdom."** A husband and wife who have come from different families, experiences, training, etc., can find wisdom between themselves if they will consider each other's points of view. But, if by pride, they reject the other individual and their perspective, there will be conflict. Proverbs 11:2 adds to this concept by saying, **"When pride cometh, then cometh shame: but with the lowly is wisdom."** James 3:14-16 gives a description of earthly or human wisdom when it says, *"But if ye have bitter envying and strife in your hearts, glory not, and lie not against the truth. This wisdom descendeth not from above, but is earthly, sensual, devilish. For where envying and strife is, there is confusion and every evil work."* Earthly wisdom is based on man's pride and individuality rather than humility and unity.

Verse 17 provides a description of heavenly wisdom by saying, *"But the wisdom that is from above is first pure, then peaceable, gentle, and easy to be intreated, full of mercy and good fruits, without partiality, and without hypocrisy."* Heavenly wisdom is always based on purity, and always seek for peace. It is careful in its actions and always ready to listen. It is consistently merciful with the goal of always doing good. It never maintains favorites and never misrepresents itself. When a couple, in biblical love, works together by listening and considering their different viewpoints (coupled with God's Word) that come from different backgrounds, experiences, dreams, etc., they can have loving unity and great wisdom in the choices they make together.

❤ *Are we dedicated to allow our differences to better our relationship rather than cause division?*

Life's Difficulties

Another major catalyst of marriage conflict is difficulties, or crises of any size or from any source. External events, circumstances, and people can put a lot of pressure on the couple. They may begin to experience difficulties with a job, finances, health, family, etc. God's desire is that these situations would draw them closer to Himself as a couple and as individuals (Romans 8:28-29, I Peter 1:5-9), as well as to each other (Philippians 3:10–Paul's relationship with Jesus grew by drawing closer through the *"fellowship of suffering"*). Satan's desire is that there would be a wedge placed in their relationship which would cause division and destruction.

King Solomon explained unity during difficulty as a necessity when he said, ***"Two are better than one; because they have a good reward for their labour. For if they fall, the one will lift up his fellow: but woe to him that is alone when he falleth; for he hath not another to help him up. Again, if two lie together, then they have heat: but how can one be warm alone? And if one prevail against him, two shall withstand him; and a threefold cord is not quickly broken"*** (Ecclesiastes 4:9-11). Each difficulty a Christian couple encounters should draw them closer to God. And through their experiences together they should grow in their love, respect and trust of each other.

❤ *Are we dedicated to accept the pressures of life together and to work in unity while depending on God for His will to be accomplished?*

*When external or internal, large or small pressure is placed on a couple and they do not maintain their proper view of God, proper control of their pride, and proper respect for each other's roles in the relationship, then sin will be produced and division will follow.

❧Relationship Building Questions☙
Article VII

1. What are some temptations from Satan that may cause you as a couple to doubt God?
   a. _____
   b. _____
   c. _____
   d. _____
   e. _____

2. What are some areas in which pride could cause conflict in a marriage?
   a. _____
   b. _____
   c. _____
   d. _____
   e. _____

3. What are the biblical roles of a husband and wife?
   a. Husband: _____
   b. Wife: _____

4. What are some ways that shame reveals itself?
   a. _____
   b. _____
   c. _____
   d. _____
   e. _____

5. What could be some signs of "covering up?"
   a. _____
   b. _____
   c. _____
   d. _____
   e. _____

♥The Conflict in the Marriage Covenant♥

6. Who can you rely on for godly wisdom and teaching for your marriage?
   a. _____
   b. _____
   c. _____
   d. _____
   e. _____
   *Are you willing to talk to these individuals now to let them know that you would desire their godly wisdom in the future?

7. Why might a couple not seek help when they are going through tough times?
   a. _____
   b. _____
   c. _____

8. How can you encourage each other to grow closer to God on a daily basis?
   a. _____
   b. _____
   c. _____
   d. _____
   e. _____

9. What are some common phrases used in "blame-shifting?"
   a. _____
   b. _____
   c. _____
   d. _____
   e. _____

♥The Conflict in the Marriage Covenant♥

10. What are some differences in your personalities?

Husband	Wife
_____	_____
_____	_____
_____	_____
_____	_____
_____	_____

What are some differences in your appetites?

Husband	Wife
_____	_____
_____	_____
_____	_____
_____	_____
_____	_____

What are some differences in your hobbies?

Husband	Wife
_____	_____
_____	_____
_____	_____
_____	_____
_____	_____

What are some differences in your use of money?

Husband	Wife
_____	_____
_____	_____
_____	_____
_____	_____
_____	_____

❤The Conflict in the Marriage Covenant❤

What are some differences in your families?

Husband	Wife
_____	_____
_____	_____
_____	_____
_____	_____

Take time to discus these differences in order to work out any conflicts before they arise.

11. What are some realistic life circumstances which could put pressure on your marriage?
    (What are some realistic life circumstances which you have seen in other marriages?)
    a. _____
    b. _____
    c. _____
    d. _____
    e. _____

Take some time to discuss how you, as a couple, can work through each of these possible situations for the glory of God and to produce greater unity in your marriage.

5 Stages of Accepting New Things

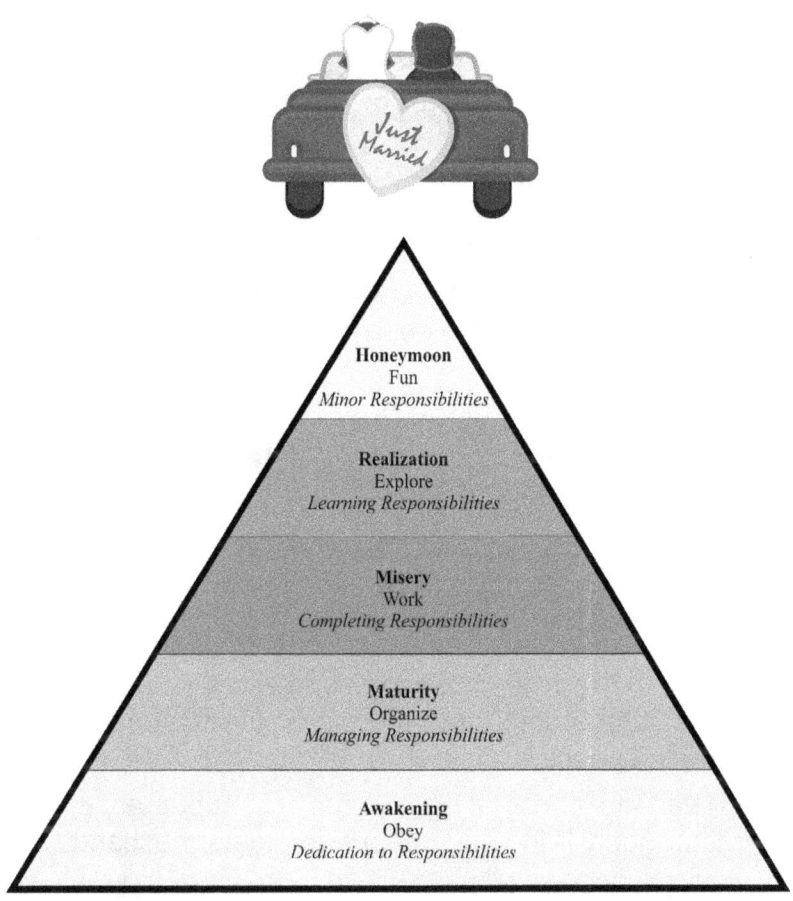

*Each stage's length may depend on the personality of each individual.

*Each stage's length and intensity may be affected by specific influences and events which impact the couple.

*Adapted from materials presented in the Christian Family class, Dr. Wynne Kimbrough, NBBC, 1996, page 38-39. Used by permission.

Keeping the Peace
I Peter 3:8-12
Romans 12:9-21

I Peter 3:11b
let him seek peace, and ensue it.

Romans 12:18
If it be possible,
as much as lieth in you,
live peaceably with all men.

*I Peter 3:1-7 teaches husbands and wives how they can make a spiritual impact in the life of their spouse while keeping the peace.

**The wife is not to use words nor appearance, but rather godly living and submission to her husband.

**The husband is not to use force, but rather pay attention to her and treat his wife tenderly.

*Romans 12:9-21 begins by saying, "**Let love be without dissimulation**" and continues by teaching how biblical love can prevent the division of relationships.

- ♥ Keeping the peace requires ... (I Peter 3:8)
    - ✎ Being of one mind - Being in agreement
        - *Romans 12:16 **Be of the same mind one toward another. Mind not high things, but condescend**

to men of low estate. Be not wise in your own conceits.

- Having compassion one to another - Suffering together

    *Romans 12:15 **Rejoice with them that do rejoice, and weep with them that weep.**

- Loving as brethren - Loving as family

    *Romans 12:10 **Be kindly affectioned one to another with brotherly love; in honour preferring one another;**

- Being pitiful - Being sympathetic

    *Romans 12:12 **Rejoicing in hope; patient in tribulation; continuing instant in prayer;**

- Being courteous - Being kind (in action)

    *Romans 12:13 **Distributing to the necessity of saints; given to hospitality.**

♥ Keeping the peace is restrictive ... (I Peter 3:9-11)

- Does no evil for evil (actions) (9a, 11a)

    "**eschew evil, and do good**"

    *Romans 12:9, 17a, 19-21

    9 Let love be without dissimulation. Abhor that which is evil; cleave to that which is good.

    17 Recompense to no man evil for evil. Provide things honest in the sight of all men.

    19 Dearly beloved, avenge not yourselves, but rather give place unto wrath: for it is written, Vengeance is mine; I will repay, saith the Lord.

    20 Therefore if thine enemy hunger, feed him; if he thirst, give him drink: for in so doing thou shalt heap coals of fire on his head.

    21 Be not overcome of evil, but overcome evil with good.

- 📎 Does not rail for railing (words) (9b, 10b)

  "*let him refrain his tongue from evil, and his lips that they speak no guile:* "

  *Does offer blessing while receiving railing

  *Romans 12:14 **Bless them which persecute you: bless, and curse not.**

  ... let him seek peace, and ensue it.
  (I Corinthians 12:14-27, Ephesians 5:22-33)

- ♥ Keeping the peace is rewarding (I Peter 3:12)
  - 📎 An inheritance of blessing
  - 📎 A life full of good days
  - 📎 A life cared for by God
    - ✓ He watches their life
    - ✓ He listens to their prayers

The Common Catalysts
&
Counsel for Marriage Conflict

*In each situation and decision which a Christian couple encounters, they must maintain their God-given roles and biblical love one for another.

The Past

1. Past family experiences and traditions (Genesis 2:24)
   a. A proper evaluation of family experiences must be made to make sure that the experiences and lessons learned are all Bible-based.
      i. By recognizing wrong experiences, the couple can prepare themselves to do right.
      ii. By recognizing right experiences, the couple can make a plan to follow the example.
   b. A realization that traditions are simply habits and patterns which may need to be eliminated, changed, or merged in order to form a new home.
      Judges 6:25-32 - Sometimes removing family traditions may come at a price, but it is an expense God will bless if done for Him.
2. Past sin and the fruit of that sin (Psalm 32, 51, Matthew 6:12-15, Galatians 6:7-8)
   a. Past sin must be confessed before God and made right before man. (Psalm 32, 51, James 5:16)
   b. Past sin must be forgiven in its entirety, and must not be used in the future as a weapon of manipulation. (Matthew 6:12-15)
   c. Past sin must be accepted as wrong but forgiven, with no lingering guilt after forgiveness and restoration has been given. (Psalm 103:12, Romans 8:1, 33-34, I John 1:9, 3:20-21)

d. Past sin must be recognized as an area of future temptation, and avoided. (Proverbs 22:3, 27:12)
e. The fruit of past sin must be accepted humbly, with a dependence on God for His mercy. (Galatians 6:7-8)

Family & Friends
(Genesis 2:23-25)

1. Family and friends must never be given first place.
2. Family and friends must be removed from having authority over the new couple.
3. Family and friends should never be valued more than each other.
4. Family and friends should not dictate the delegation of the couple's time (although their desires may be considered in any decision-making process—holidays, vacations, etc.)
5. Family and friends should never be a used to "blow-off steam." A husband and wife must never speak poorly about their spouse to others. (Family and friends will begin to think incorrectly about the spouse because they heard of the difficultly but never the kissing and making up afterward.) (Proverbs 17:9)

Children

1. The number of children should be discussed and agreed on based on all of the couple's circumstances along with a diligent search for God's will. (Proverbs 127:5)
2. The provision of children should be accepted as God's right and not a manipulation of man's science. (Psalm 127:3)

3. The provision of healthy or sick children should not diminish the joy of God's blessing on them as a couple, and should be seen as God's perfect, loving plan for the couple by His entrusting them with a precious soul to raise for His glory. (Exodus 4:10-11)
4. The raising and discipline of children should always be based on and faithful to clear biblical teaching. (Proverbs 13:24, 22:6, 15, 29:15, Ephesians 6:4, Colossians 3:21)
    a. The husband must be the leader in the raising of the children.
    b. The husband and wife should discuss the biblical standards of and practical application for the discipline of their children.
    c. The husband and wife must be seen as equals by the children and support each other in front of their children at all times.

Finances/Provisions

1. Spending/Savings
    a. An understanding that all that they have belongs to and is provided by God must be reached and remembered. (I Chronicles 29:11-12, I Timothy 6:17)
    b. A joyful practice of honoring God through tithes and offerings must be consistently maintained. (Malachi 3:8-9, II Corinthians 9:6-12)
    c. A realistic budget should be established and followed.
    d. Discontentment must be rejected and contentment must be achieved. (Luke 12:15-21, I Timothy 6:5-6, Hebrews 13:5)
    e. Debt must be viewed as dangerous and must be avoided when at all possible. (Proverbs 22:7)

- f. Anything gained or earned by either the husband or wife should be shared for the benefit of the entire family. (Proverbs 31:10-31)

    *One individual may be in charge of actually paying the bills, but both should always be aware of what is going on.
- g. Constant communication about the finances should be maintained so that the husband and wife can both make wise decisions about any purchases they make.
- h. Savings should be practiced when possible, but never depended on at the sacrifice of trusting God. (Proverbs 22:3, 23:5, Matthew 6:19-21, I Timothy 6:17)

2. Housing
    - a. All housing and possessions (appliances, furniture, etc.) must be seen as God's provision and the couple must be content with what God has given them. (I Timothy 6:8-10)
    - b. The husband must provide the best he can for adequate, secure, and comfortable housing for his wife. (I Timothy 5:7)
    - c. The wife must recognize that she is keeping the home for her husband and therefore should seek to please him with how she sets it up and maintains it. (Genesis 2:18, 20-23, Proverbs 31:11, 28)

3. Jobs
    - a. The man should be seen as the bread-winner, therefore his job must determine the location of the family. (Where God sends the man, he sends the family.) (I Timothy 5:8, Genesis 12:1-5)
    - b. The man should seek to balance his work in such a way that there is no damage to his family responsibilities. (Deuteronomy 24:5, I Corinthians 7:33-34)

c. The wife's first responsibility must be seen as her home. When this responsibility is maintained, she should defer to her husband's counsel and wishes about working outside the home. (Proverbs 31:10-31, Titus 2:4-5)

d. Neither the husband or wife should wrongly sacrifice "time" with the family by working to gain "things" for the family. (Things never replace time and relationships!)

Physical intimacy

A much more detailed review of this subject will be presented in the final lesson on "Fulfilment in the Marriage Covenant."

1. Misunderstanding - The husband and wife must accept that God has created physical intimacy to be His perfect plan for pleasure in the Marriage Covenant. Although physical intimacy outside of marriage is sin and always produces guilt, physical unity and fulfilment within marriage is approved of, encouraged, and blessed by God in the husband and wife relationship. (Genesis 1:26-31, I Corinthians 7:1-5, Hebrews 13:4)

2. Past relationships - A husband or wife who has been involved in other relationships through dating, engagement, or physical relationships will carry their memories and experiences into their new marriage. These previous relationships have been a part of shaping who they presently are, both for the good and the bad. For those relationships which have included sin, there may be guilt and shame. However, God desires that through confession the guilt be removed (I John 1:9), and that through honesty and transparency in confession, the shame will not cause any future damage (Luke 8:17). As well, any past relationship must be removed from being a source of comparison.

Although there may have been exhilarating experiences in the past, they were all sinful and contrary to God's perfect plan in the marriage (Proverbs 9:17-18, Hebrews 11:25b).

3. Lack of education (I Peter 3:7) - A husband and wife who have not had extensive medical training often have a difficult time understanding how perfectly and wonderfully God created their bodies. The man's and woman's anatomies are created extremely different, and many of the sexual organs which provide true sexual pleasure are located in discrete, protected areas of the body. For this reason, it is important that each marriage partner help the other know their body by communication and exploration, and that when available, both of them look at good, educational materials about one another's bodies so that they can truly understand how to fulfill the desires of their spouse. Also, there should be no shame in discussing any questions or concerns with a medical professional if the need should arise (they are trained and understand the human anatomy).

4. Frequency (I Corinthians 7:2-5) - A husband and wife should never refuse their spouse the privilege of physical intimacy for any extended period of time. God has created physical intimacy in marriage to be the protection from sexual sin, and He warns against the attack of temptation when proper sexual fulfilment in marriage is not enjoyed. However, there must also be a loving understanding of each other's time, energy, health, etc. God is clear that each spouse should "give" to their spouse but there must never be "demanding" or "taking."

5. Unfulfilled expectations (Proverbs 13:12, I Corinthians 7:2-5) - A husband and wife may have their own ideas about physical intimacy. One may be adventurous while the other is apprehensive, or one may be more aggressive while the other is timid. For this reason it is very important that biblical love is expressed while "love

making" is practiced (I Corinthians 13:4-8a). A husband and wife must have realistic expectations of each other and reject the world's advertisement of intimacy and pleasure. Satan is the master counterfeiter and liar. He will always make things look different than what God says they are. Proper physical intimacy is like a jigsaw puzzle: although the box presents a beautiful picture as an advertisement, and that same picture is inside the box, the picture inside the box needs much work, patience, and coordination in order to come together correctly. But when the puzzle is completed and all the pieces fit together, the joy and satisfaction are wonderful.

Discovering Differences

Here is a list of helpful questions to help you learn not only why your future spouse is who he/she is but also to learn what will be expected of you.

Take some time to investigate your differences and discuss the reasons for each one. Then, determine the best way to compromise for your future.

Family life (and relationships)
- What marital example do your parents provide?
- What influence do your siblings have in your family?
- What were the living conditions in your home growing up (poor, middle class, wealthy)?
- What friends have influence over you?

Spiritual life
- When did you accept Jesus Christ as your personal Savior?
- When were you baptized?
- What church(es) did you attend growing up?
- In what church ministries have you participated or served?
- What are your current personal spiritual habits?
    - Daily devotions
    - Prayer time
    - Evangelism
    - Tithing
    - Other

Family Dreams
- How many children would you like to have?
- How often would you like to spend time with your parents?
- Where would you like to spend your holidays?
- What are some family traditions you would like to maintain in your home?

Future Dreams
- Where would you like to live?
- What vocation would you like to have?
- What type of home would you like to own?
- What type of car would you like to drive?
- What type of gifts would please you?
- Would you like to have pets?

Living habits
- What time do you wake up and go to sleep?
- How do you prefer to drive (fast, slow, etc.)?
- What type of food do you prefer to eat?
- What are your color preferences?
- What is our preferred temperature?
- What are your home decor preferences?
- What hobbies would you like to enjoy?
- What political views do you hold?

Living expectations
- How should minor and major car and home repairs be taken care of (hang pictures, change oil, leaky sink, etc.)?

- Whose job is it ...?
    - Take out the trash
    - Cook
    - Wash the dishes
    - Clean the house
    - Do the laundry
    - Pump the gas
    - Cut the grass
    - Go shopping
    - Maintain the finances
- What should we do about the little things that make a big difference?
    - The direction of the toilet paper roll
    - The amount of time spent in the bathroom
    - Arriving early or late
    - Squeezing of the toothpaste (top, middle, bottom)
    - Organize your belongings
    - Table manners
    - Personal noises
- What if ...?
    - We have an argument
    - We can't have children
    - We have a child with handicaps
    - We lose our job
    - One of us becomes seriously ill
    - We need to move from our family, friends, and church
    - We become wealthy

Monthly Budgeting

Husband's Income _____ Wife's Income _____
Total Income _____

	Expenses	Budget	Cost	Difference
Housing	House/Rent			
	Electric			
	Water			
	Garbage			
	Insurance			
	Maint/Misc			
	Phone			
	Cable/Internet			
	Furniture			
	Taxes			
	Housing Total	$	$	$

	Expenses	Budget	Cost	Diference
Salary	Tithe			
	Food			
	Clothing			
	Medical Cost			
	Eye/Dental			
	Cell Phone			
	Tuition			
	Vehicle			
	Misc.			
	Salary Total	$	$	$

Chapter 8

Article VIII
The Restoration of the Marriage Covenant
Genesis 3:6-9, 12-13, 16-24, 4:1-2

In the restoration of a relationship, both parties must participate. In Genesis 3, Adam and Eve sinned against God, and the pattern of how man tries to cover his sin and how God properly deals with sin were revealed. A marriage relationship must be built on dealing with sin rather than simply covering it up.

Genesis 3:6 says, *"And when the woman saw that the tree was good for food, and that it was pleasant to the eyes, and a tree to be desired to make one wise, she took of the fruit thereof, and did eat, and gave also unto her husband with her; and he did eat."* Immediately following their sin the Bible says, *"And the eyes of them both were opened, and they knew that they were naked; and they sewed fig leaves together, and made themselves apron"* (Genesis 3:7). Adam and Eve experienced something God never intended for them to experience. Their sin gave them knowledge of things that were wrong and dangerous. Their sin also produced feelings they had never experienced before. They found themselves ashamed to be together in perfect openness and harmony. Their shame motivated them to make something they had not previously needed and they tried to cover themselves with makeshift clothing. Their marriage relationship was being destroyed because of their sin. They had violated God's standards and found themselves out of fellowship with each other. The same is true for each marriage in which sin is allowed to enter. There will be an unholy knowledge of things which are wrong, and shame and secretism will develop. If left unattended, the distance between the husband and wife will grow until the marriage is broken.

♥The Restoration of the Marriage Covenant♥

Confront the Conflicts Daily

Immediately following Adam and Eve's sin and attempt to cover their shame *"they heard the voice of the LORD God walking in the garden in the cool of the day"* (Genesis 3:8). It is apparent that on the very same day that Adam and Eve sinned, God came looking to confront and resolve the conflict. God did not desire for there to be division between them and knew the danger which would come if they continued in their sinful ways. Ephesians 4:26-27 says, *"Be ye angry, and sin not: let not the sun go down upon your wrath: Neither give place to the devil."* This biblical mandate must be adopted by every married couple that desires God's protect from Satanic attack on their marriage. When an issue arises, they must commit to each other to resolve it as soon as possible (the very same day) so that there is no opportunity for doubt of commitment or bitterness.

♥ *Are we committed to resolve every conflict in our marriage as quickly as possible so as to keep our relationship protected from the attacks of Satan?*

Don't Make Excuses

Genesis 3:8-9 continues the story, *"And they heard the voice of the LORD God walking in the garden in the cool of the day: and Adam and his wife hid themselves from the presence of the LORD God amongst the trees of the garden. And the LORD God called unto Adam, and said unto him, Where art thou?"* God came looking for their fellowship and they ran from Him. God, already knowing Adam and Eve's sin and where they were, began His confrontation with a question, *"Where art thou?"* Adam responded to God's question by saying, *"I heard thy voice in the garden, and I was afraid, because I was naked; and I hid myself*" (Genesis 3:10). God, still all knowing, continued with His convicting questions by asking *"Who told thee that thou wast naked? Hast thou eaten of the tree, whereof I commanded thee that thou shouldest not eat?"* God confronted Adam directly with his own confession. Adam attempted to distract God from the real problem. He focused on the fruit of their sin rather than confessing their sin. But God saw through the bluff and got to the root of the sin, which was their lack of faith in God's Word and rebellion against God's commandment by eating the forbidden fruit (James 1:12-15).

Sadly, Adam displayed the pattern found most often in the marriage relationship–making excuses and blame shifting. Instead of accepting his fault, he attempted to pass the responsibility on to Eve when he said *"The woman whom thou gavest to be with me, she gave me of the tree, and I did eat"* (Genesis 3:12). Adam attempted to directly blame Eve for his sin and indirectly blame God. Eve followed the leadership of her husband as she responded to God's convicting question by saying, *"The serpent beguiled me, and I did eat"* (Genesis 3:13).

❤ *Are we committed to not make excuses or blame shift when we have done wrong?*

Deal With the Seed

Although Adam and Eve both attempted to excuse themselves from their guilt, God dealt with them directly about their true sin. As God presented the punishment for their sin, He eliminated their excuses. Specifically for Adam, God used his excuse against him in his judgement as He said, *"Because thou hast hearkened unto the voice of thy wife, and hast eaten of the tree, of which I commanded thee, saying, Thou shalt not eat of it ...*" (Genesis 3:17). God was very clear about their personal responsibility for their sin as he punished each one specifically and individually. God is not fooled by excuses or by the fruit of sin. He desires to get to the seed of the sin so that it does not return like a stubborn weed. Proverbs 13:10 says, **"Only by pride cometh contention: but with the well advised is wisdom."** The seed of conflict is always pride (self-focus). Pride may be revealed in different ways by different people as it takes root and grows, but it will ways produce conflict in the end. For Adam and Eve their pride of trusting their own understanding and following their own desires developed roots and grew as they rejected what they were specifically commanded by God and sinned. But **"by humility and the fear of the LORD are riches, and honour, and life"** (Proverbs 22:4). James 1:12-15 shares the process of sin by saying, **"Blessed is the man that endureth temptation: for when he is tried, he shall receive the crown of life, which the Lord hath promised to them that love him. Let no man say when he is tempted, I am tempted of God: for God cannot be tempted with evil, neither tempteth he any man: but every man is tempted, when he is drawn away of his own lust, and enticed. Then when lust hath conceived, it bringeth forth sin: and sin, when it is finished, bringeth forth death."** When the seed of pride takes root and produces sin each individual must follow David's confession in Psalm 51:6-12 when he said, **"Behold, thou desirest truth in the inward parts: and in the hidden part thou shalt make me to know wisdom. Purge me with hyssop, and I shall be clean: wash me, and I shall be whiter than snow. Make me to hear joy and gladness; that the bones which thou hast broken may rejoice. Hide thy face from my sins, and blot out all mine iniquities. Create in me a clean heart, O God; and renew a right spirit within me. Cast me not away from thy presence; and take not thy holy spirit from me. Restore unto me the joy of thy salvation; and uphold me with thy free spirit."** If a husband and wife do not truthfully and thoroughly deal with the seed of pride and the roots which it produces in their personal conflict they will not be clean in their *"heart,"* and will constantly find themselves returning to the same sin and find themselves in conflict.

❤ *Are we committed to take the time and effort to deal with the seed of our conflict so that the fruit of sin does not continually return?*

Definitively Forgive

During God's proclamation of Satan's punishment, God presented His long-term plan for Adam and Eve's cleansing from their sin when he said, *"And I will put enmity between thee and the woman, and between thy seed and her seed; it shall bruise thy head, and thou shalt bruise his heel"* (Genesis 3:15). Thankfully, through Jesus Christ, all of man's sin has been paid for (I John 2:1-2). God also expressed His care for Adam and Eve's immediate need, and dealt with their present sin and shame. God did not let time pass, but dealt immediately with the situation (Ephesians 4:26-27). He lovingly made *"coats of skins, and clothed them"* (Genesis 3:21). God sacrificed one of his pure, newly created animals to lovingly display His forgiveness and continued care for their needs. True forgiveness between a husband and wife will follow God's example. Ephesians 4:31-32 commands, *"Let all bitterness, and wrath, and anger, and clamour, and evil speaking, be put away from you, with all malice: and be ye kind one to another, tenderhearted, forgiving one another, even as God for Christ's sake hath forgiven you."* Psalm 103:12 explains the extensiveness of God's forgiveness by saying, *"As far as the east is from the west, so far hath he removed our transgressions from us."* For *"hatred stirreth up strifes: but love covereth all sins"* (Proverbs 10:12). When I John 1:9 presents God's plan for repentance and forgiveness, it promises that, *"If we confess our sins, he is faithful and just to forgive us our sins, and to cleanse us from all unrighteousness."* In a Marriage Covenant, the husband and wife must be committed to follow the same pattern. They must first set aside their pride to ask for forgiveness, and when forgiveness is requested, they must be faithful and just in their provision of forgiveness. They must show true love by forgiving each other and continuing a united relationship. Only when "love" follows the biblical definition found in I Corinthians 13:4-8 can true forgiveness by given. For love (charity) *"suffereth long, and is kind; charity envieth not; charity vaunteth not itself, is not puffed up, doth not behave itself unseemly, seeketh not her own, is not easily provoked, thinketh no evil; rejoiceth not in iniquity, but rejoiceth in the truth; beareth all things, believeth all things, hopeth all things, endureth all things. Charity never faileth ..."* (I Corinthians 13:4-8). God's love for mankind has made a way through the blood of Jesus Christ to cover, or forgive, each and every sin committed when, by faith, we accept His work on the Cross. This same type of love must be expressed in the Marriage Covenant. At times forgiveness may come at great expense due to the great pain caused. However, our example of love is God, and He says *"And above all things have fervent charity [love] among yourselves: for charity [love] shall cover the multitude of sins"* (I Peter 4:8).

❤ *Are we committed to totally forgive when we have been wronged?*

Determine to Restore

Adam and Eve faced God's punishment (Genesis 3:16-19) and the fruit of their sin (Genesis 3:22-24) as they faced the rest of their lives together, but they were determined to be together.

Genesis 3:20 reveals Adam's commitment to Eve in their one flesh relationship as he *"called his wife's name Eve; because she was the mother of all living."* As of yet, Eve had not had a child. God had just prophesied of a Savior through Eve's giving birth. Adam, being the spiritual leader of the couple, chose to express his faith in God's new plan by renaming Woman as Eve. However, Adam and Eve would still need to live together according to their Marriage Covenant in order for this prophesy to be fulfilled. It was not enough for each individual partner to be right with God alone, they needed to be right with each other and together. Genesis 4:1-2 reveals that Adam and Eve were continually together as it reports, *"And Adam knew Eve his wife; and she conceived, and bare Cain, and said, I have gotten a man from the LORD. And she again bare his brother Abel. And Abel was a keeper of sheep, but Cain was a tiller of the ground."* Adam and Eve faced difficult times because of sin, but following the correction from God they returned to their marriage relationship and no longer held each other to blame for their situation. In unity they faced the consequences (fruit) of their sin, while focusing on God and His promise from that day forward.

When a husband and wife have experienced marital conflict and have worked together to find the seed problem and roots which have developed, expressed proper repentance, and have forgiven each other, they must return to their dedicated and loving relationship as if the conflict never had existed. Revelation 2:2-5 provides God's counsel for those who have *"left their first love."* The context is directly related to a church and Jesus Christ, but gives principles which can be used in matrimony. Verses 2 and 3 give praise to their outward dedication to the relationship. It says, *"I know thy works, and thy labour, and thy patience, and how thou canst not bear them which are evil: and thou hast tried them which say they are apostles, and are not, and hast found them liars: And hast borne, and hast patience, and for my name's sake hast laboured, and hast not fainted."* In marriage, this would be similar to the husband not failing to fulfill his job of taking out the garbage, repairing the car, etc., and for the wife that she was cooking, cleaning, etc. Verse 4 displays a sad truth about the relationship. It says, *"Nevertheless I have somewhat against thee, because thou hast left thy first love."* Although all of the outward practices were correct, the inward heart was not. Within matrimony, a husband and wife can live in the same home and share the same belongings, and yet be very cold one toward another. God did not want this type of relationship for the Bride of Christ (the church), and He does not want it for the bride and groom in the Marriage Covenant. For this reason He prescribes a solution in verse 5, which says, *"Remember therefore from whence thou art fallen, and repent, and do the first works ..."* A husband and wife who have found themselves in marriage conflict must first remember their relationship before the conflict arose. They must remember their covenant one to another. Second, they must repent of how they have sinned and lived outside of biblical love. And third, they must return to living lovingly with each other and enjoying each other's companionship.

❤ *Are we committed to work together to restore our love for each other and our relationship following any controversy?*

What about ...

The sad question must be asked, "What about when one of the marriage partners does not wish to get right?" This situation may be found at any number of levels. There are times when resistance lasts for a few hours, and others for years. However, with God, the time of the resistance is not important. His solution is found in I Peter 3:1-7. I Peter 3:1 says, *"... if any obey not the word, they also may without the word be won ..."* Specifically, Peter is addressing the wife in this verse, but the principle is universal. A husband or wife whose spouse is knowingly living contrary to God's Word is not to attack, badger or nag their spouse. They are to focus on being consistently godly in their personal life and obedient to their God-given roles and responsibilities in front of the spouse while trusting God to produce the conviction and change He desires in His way and time. Specifically, the wife is instructed *"Likewise, ye wives, be in subjection to your own husbands; that, if any obey not the word, they also may without the word be won by the conversation of the wives; while they behold your chaste conversation coupled with fear. Whose adorning let it not be that outward adorning of plaiting the hair, and of wearing of gold, or of putting on of apparel; but let it be the hidden man of the heart, in that which is not corruptible, even the ornament of a meek and quiet spirit, which is in the sight of God of great price. For after this manner in the old time the holy women also, who trusted in God, adorned themselves, being in subjection unto their own husbands: even as Sara obeyed Abraham, calling him lord: whose daughters ye are, as long as ye do well, and are not afraid with any amazement."* A godly wife will live in subjection and honor of her husband just as Sarah obeyed Abraham (Genesis 17:15-25:10). She will stay focused on living a life which is inwardly beautiful and displayed in an outward spirit of meekness and quietness. As time passes, she will not become discouraged or disappointed because she will not fear her husband or his disobedience, but rather depend on God for her protection and provision. For the husband, God's instruction is, *"Likewise, ye husbands, dwell with them according to knowledge, giving honour unto the wife, as unto the weaker vessel, and as being heirs together of the grace of life; that your prayers be not hindered."* Although a husband cannot force his wife to submit to God's authority, he is to love her with his entire life. He is to treat her honorably, as a precious gift from God (Proverbs 18:22), and he is to remember that they are spiritually equal before God. By doing so, he will display a

♥The Restoration of the Marriage Covenant♥

daily picture of Jesus Christ's love to his wife which the Holy Spirit can use to draw her back to Himself.

✦Relationship Building Questions✦
Article VIII

1. What are the three results of sin?
   a. _____
   b. _____
   c. _____

2. What are some excuses which might be used in a marriage conflict?
   a. _____
   b. _____
   c. _____
   d. _____

3. What might be the seed/root of the following controversies?
   a. <u>Spending Money -</u> _____
   b. _____
   c. _____
   d. _____

4. What are some ways to show that forgiveness has been given?
   a. _____
   b. _____
   c. _____
   d. _____

5. What are some ways that a husband and wife can return to their loving relationship after a conflict?
   a. _____
   b. _____
   c. _____
   d. _____

6. How should a spouse respond if their husband or wife does not want to get right or do right? _____

Rekindling the Flame
Revelation 2:2-5

- ♥ Love is not found in <u>actions</u> alone (2-4)
  *I Corinthians 13:1-3
  - ✎ Good <u>works</u> do not guarantee true love
  - ✎ <u>Separation</u> from others does not guarantee true love
  - ✎ <u>Patience</u> in trials does not guarantee true love

- ♥ Love is based in a <u>decision</u> (attitude) (4)
  *I Corinthians 13:4-8
  *I Juan 3:14-18
  *Love is self-sacrificial for the benefit of the one being loved - Juan 3:16, Romans 5:8
  - ✎ The <u>husband</u> must learn to love - Ephesians 5:25-28
  - ✎ The <u>wife</u> must learn to love - Titus 2:3-5

- ♥ Love can be <u>restored</u> when it has been lost (5)
  *Proverbs 6:1-3
  - ✎ You must <u>remember</u> your attitude of dedication in the past
  - ✎ You must <u>repent</u> of the detractions of your attitude in the present
  - ✎ You must <u>return</u> to your attitude and application of dedication in the future

11 Investments for Life-Long Love from Song of Solomon

Song of Solomon 8:6-7

Set me as a seal upon thine heart, ...
for love is strong as death ...
Many waters cannot quench love,
neither can the floods drown it:
if a man would give
all the substance of his house for love,
it would utterly be contemned.

- Great your spouse with a kiss and consider your spouses kisses as a sweet treat (1:2, 4:11, 7:9)
- Reminisce about the joy of being with your spouse in the past and anxiously anticipate your next encounter (1:4)
- Share your daily schedule and plans with your spouse (1:7)
- Appreciate and praise your spouse's appearance and fragrance (privately and publicly) (1:9-17 4:1-9, 5:9-16, 6:4-10, 7:1-9)
- Regularly and tenderly embrace your spouse (2:6, 8:3)
- Allow your spouse to get good rest (2:7, 3:5, 8:4)
- Know and enjoy your spouses voice and look forward to conversing together (2:8)
- Look for opportunities to get away with your spouse (2:9-15)
- Diligently seek to quickly correct any misunderstandings or differences that cause a separation from your spouse (3:1-2, 5:1-8)
- Delight in every aspect of sensuality and intercourse with your spouse and let them know how much they please you (1:13b, 3:4, 4:9-16, 5:1, 6:11-13, 7:1-13, 8:1-3)

- Constantly affirm your exclusive relationship with your spouse (privately and publically) and reassure them that no one else compares to them (2:1-3, 16, 5:9-16, 6:3, 7:10, 8:10b)

Chapter 9

Article IX
The Expansion of the Marriage Covenant
Genesis 1:28, 4:1-2

God, immediately after creating Adam and Eve, blessed them and *"said unto them, Be fruitful, and multiply, and replenish the earth, and subdue it ..."* (Genesis 1:28). God's design for mankind to reproduce future generations is directly connected to the Marriage Covenant. It is His perfect plan that families would grow out of the husband and wife relationship and that their children would continue to follow their parent's example of raising families so that the entire earth would be plentiful with human life. God's design requires unity between the husband and wife, a unity to have children and a unity to raise their children. They must both be unified in their dependence upon God and their dedication to God by saying *"as for me and my house, we will serve the LORD"* (Joshua 24:15).

Unity which Produces Children

Adam and Eve experienced the physical union through the *"one flesh"* relationship which is encouraged and blessed by God (Genesis 2:23-25, Hebrews 13:4). As they enjoyed this intimacy, the Bible says, *"And Adam knew Eve his wife; and she conceived, and bare Cain, and said, I have gotten a man from the LORD. And she again bare his brother Abel. And Abel was a keeper of sheep, but Cain was a tiller of the ground"* (Genesis 4:1-2). The extended blessing of a husband's and wife's commitment to and enjoyment of their Marriage Covenant is the production of a physical representation of their union together through a new life being produced in a little child. What a wonderful design God has provided! God had promised Adam and Eve children as He said to Eve, *"I will greatly multiply thy sorrow and thy conception; in sorrow thou shalt bring forth children"* (Genesis 3:16). *"And Adam called his wife's name Eve; because she was the mother of all living"* (Genesis 3:20). Each Christian couple does not have the same promise, but they can depend on the same design. As they are unified in their relationship and wait for God's specific and loving will for their lives, they can trust that He will provide them with the exact children He knows are best for them. And they can say with Adam and Eve, *"I have gotten a man [child] from the LORD"* (Genesis 4:1). Psalms 127:3 say, *"Lo, children are an heritage of the LORD: and the fruit of the womb is his reward."* Therefore, a husband and wife should be grateful to God for each child He provides, and be prudent with their abilities and efforts in training each of them in accordance to God's Word.

Genesis 4:2 reveals an important principle which must be recognized by each Christian couple as it says, *"... And Abel was a keeper of sheep, but Cain was a tiller of the ground."* Although God has established a universal program for producing children, He never relinquishes His creative control to the parents. Although Abel and Cain came from the same parents, they were both very different individuals and served very different roles throughout life. As a Christian couple seeks God's provision and timing for having children, they must recognize the personal and particular creative process which God is accomplishing in the womb as He forms a specific baby for them to enjoy. The Psalmist said it this way, *"For thou hast possessed my reins: thou hast covered me in my mother's womb. I will praise thee; for I am fearfully and wonderfully made: marvellous are thy works; and that my soul knoweth right well. My substance was not hid from thee, when I was made in secret, and curiously wrought in the lowest parts of the earth. Thine eyes did see my substance, yet being unperfect; and in thy book all my members were written, which in continuance were fashioned, when as yet there was none of them"* (Psalm 139:13-16).

God is a very specific creator, and has a very specific plan for each child He creates (Genesis 25:20-27). A Christian couple should depend on Him for the color of their baby's hair and eyes. They should equally depend on Him for their baby's health and abilities (Exodus 4:11). And if God lovingly chooses for their child to have life-altering difficulties, they must remember Jesus' loving answer to His disciples as they asked, *"Master, who did sin, this man, or his parents, that he was born blind? Jesus answered, Neither hath this man sinned, nor his parents: but that the works of God should be made manifest in him"* (John 9:2-3). Each child is created for the specific purpose of bringing glory to their Creator.

If God, in His perfect, loving will, chooses that the couple should face a difficult pregnancy, miscarriage, or the inability to have children, they must, by faith, trust God to work perfectly on their behalf. They must remember the example of Abraham and Sarah and realize that God has a very special plan for their family, a plan which would display His power and glory if they do not attempt to take matters into their own hands (Genesis 16:1-17:19). During this difficult time, they must comfort each other as David comforted Bathsheba after the death of their son (II Samuel 12:24). They must depend on *"the Father of mercies, and the God of all comfort; Who comforteth us in all our tribulation, that we may be able to comfort them which are in any trouble, by the comfort wherewith we ourselves are comforted of God"* (II Corinthians 1:3-4).

Regardless of the circumstances surrounding a pregnancy and birth of a child, a Christian young couple must follow the example of Moses' parents as they *"by faith"* tried to protect him, but when the circumstances became out of human control, they *"by faith"* trusted God to do what was best (Exodus 2:1-10, Hebrews 11:23). The blessing they received was beyond human imagination as Moses was returned to them to raise as an infant and toddler, and then he lived in a king's palace, where God continued to mold him to become a great leader of God's chosen people. The faith of Moses' parents in the midst of the most difficult times of their parenting, produced an opportunity for God's wisdom, power, and protection to be displayed to the world throughout all time. As parents, it is right to protect and provide for one's child, but as dangers of health, accidents, etc. become out of human control, each parent must place their child back into the hands of the all-loving, all-powerful, and all-wise Creator.

As a Christian couple desires to have children, they should follow Hannah's example as she *"... prayed unto the LORD ... And she vowed a vow, and said, O LORD of hosts, if thou wilt indeed look on the affliction of thine handmaid, and remember me, and not forget thine handmaid, but wilt give unto thine handmaid a man child, then I will give him unto the LORD all the days of his life ..."* (I Samuel 1:10-11). Hannah acknowledged that God was the source of all life and she promised to give back her child to Him. She accepted that in reality each soul belongs to God, and each child is simply loaned to their parents by God so that they can train him/her to glorify God with his/her life.

❤ *Are we committed to depend on God's design for having children?*

❤ *Are we committed to depend on the all-loving and all-wise Creator God to create the exact children He wants us to enjoy and train for His glory?*

❤ *Are we committed to unitedly depend on God through any difficulties we may face in pregnancy and raising our children?*

❤ *Are we committed to give our children back to God, recognizing that their primary purpose is to obey and glorify Him with their entire life?*

❤The Expansion of the Marriage Covenant❤

Unity in Parenting Children

The Bible does not record any specific accounts of how Adam and Eve raised their children. By Cain's and Able's actions of sacrificing to God, it is evident that Adam and Eve had passed their knowledge about their creator God on to their children. God's program for each new generation to learn about Him through their parents is presented throughout Scripture both by specific teaching and various examples. King Solomon said, *"Let us hear the conclusion of the whole matter: Fear God, and keep his commandments: for this is the whole duty of man. For God shall bring every work into judgment, with every secret thing, whether it be good, or whether it be evil"* (Ecclesiastes 12:13-14). He provided his son with an entire book of spiritual proverbs to encourage him to *"fear God and keep His commandments."* God is very specific in His command found in Deuteronomy 6:5-13 which says, *"And thou shalt love the LORD thy God with all thine heart, and with all thy soul, and with all thy might. And these words, which I command thee this day, shall be in thine heart: And thou shalt teach them diligently unto thy children, and shalt talk of them when thou sittest in thine house, and when thou walkest by the way, and when thou liest down, and when thou risest up. And thou shalt bind them for a sign upon thine hand, and they shall be as frontlets between thine eyes. And thou shalt write them upon the posts of thy house, and on thy gates ... Thou shalt fear the LORD thy God, and serve him, and shalt swear by his name."* Parents are responsible to *"Train up a child in the way he should go"* (Proverbs 22:6). This training must be on a daily basis and involve every area of life. One of the best descriptions for the responsibility of parents can be found in "discipleship," and the best example of discipleship is found in Jesus Christ. Jesus Christ lived with his disciples for three years. He participated in their lives and they in His, but He never neglected His leadership. He was always providing for their three essential needs: teaching, correction, and provision.

Christian parents must do the same. They must dedicate their lives to disciple the next generation which is growing up in their own home.

❤ *Are we committed to disciple our children on a daily basis based on the teaching of Scripture.*

Unity in Teaching

Jesus Christ constantly instructed his disciples. Sometimes His instruction came as preaching, sometimes as parables, sometimes as rebukes, and sometimes as simple statements about God and His ways while living through every-day events. Parenting should reflect this same method of teaching. Timothy is an example of a child who did not grow up in a "perfect" home but had the privilege of having one parent and grandparent who taught him God's Word from his youth (II Timothy 1:4). Paul reminds him of this privilege and responsibility as he says, **"*Continue thou in the things which thou hast learned and hast been assured of, knowing of whom thou hast learned them; And that from a child thou hast known the holy scriptures, which are able to make thee wise unto salvation through faith which is in Christ Jesus*"** (II Timothy 3:14-15). He then continued with the very foundation of producing godly children when he said **"*All scripture is given by inspiration of God, and is profitable for doctrine, for reproof, for correction, for instruction in righteousness: That the man of God may be perfect, throughly furnished unto all good works*"** (II Timothy 3:16-17). Christian parents who desire to have godly children must be dedicated to God's Word. They must always exalt the practicality and authority of the Bible by specifically teaching it, regularly explaining and applying it to real life situations, and consistently living it. A Christian father must be joined by his wife (help meet) as they **"*bring them [their children]* up in the nurture and** *admonition of the Lord"* (Ephesians 6:4). Christian parents must accept their responsibility of teaching their children proper doctrine, as well as showing them how to apply it to their daily life. In Titus 2 Paul gives Titus instruction about the *"sound doctrine"* he was to teach. In verses 3 through 8 he specifically stated that the older generation should be instructing the younger when he said, *"The aged women likewise, that they be ... teachers of good things; That they may teach the young women to be sober, to love their husbands, to love their children, To be discreet, chaste, keepers at home, good, obedient to their own husbands, that the word of God be not blasphemed. Young men likewise exhort to be sober minded. In all things shewing thyself a pattern of good works: in doctrine shewing uncorruptness, gravity, sincerity, Sound speech, that cannot be condemned; that he that is of the contrary part may be ashamed, having no evil thing to say of you."* These verses present God's standard for the next generation. This standard should be taught in the home and re-affirmed and enhanced by the ministry of the local church.

❤ *Are we committed to daily teach our children God's Word through spoken word and good example?*

❤ *Are we committed to teach our children not only the truths of Scripture, but also the practical application of those truths?*

Unity in Correction

On numerous occasions, Jesus Christ needed to confront and correct the actions or words of his disciples. Once, He emphatically said to Peter, **"Get thee behind me, Satan: thou art an offence unto me: for thou savourest not the things that be of God, but those that be of men"** (Matthew 16:23). Jesus Christ's direct confrontation of Peter's statements could be perceived by some as drastic, but Jesus perfectly provided correction equal to the crime. Parents face the same difficulty while disciplining their children. The world says that biblical discipline is harsh and drastic, but the Bible is very clear that, *"The rod and reproof give wisdom: but a child left to himself bringeth his mother to shame"* (Proverbs 29:15). Proper correction or disciplining of a child is of the utmost importance. Proverbs 22:15 says, *"Foolishness is bound in the heart of a child; but the rod of correction shall drive it far from him."* And Proverbs 23:13-14 adds, *"Withhold not correction from the child: for if thou beatest him with the rod, he shall not die. Thou shalt beat him with the rod, and shalt deliver his soul from hell."* The most important goal for a Christian parent must be that their child receives God's eternal salvation. God says that one important step in realizing this goal is by proper discipline. As parents discipline their child, they are not just addressing the specific wrong-doing at that time, but are also instilling in their child's heart the difference between right and wrong, and that there is always a punishment for doing wrong. Without this understanding, a child will grow up with no respect for God's holiness nor a realization of his/her need for God's forgiveness. Proverbs 13:24 is very specific, *"He that spareth his rod hateth his son: but he that loveth him chasteneth him betimes."* As parents properly correct their children, they display God's love to them (Proverbs 3:11-12). Hebrews 12:5-8 says, *"... My son, despise not thou the chastening of the Lord, nor faint when thou art rebuked of him: For whom the Lord loveth he chasteneth, and scourgeth every son whom he receiveth. If ye endure chastening, God dealeth with you as with sons; for what son is he whom the father chasteneth not? But if ye be without chastisement, whereof all are partakers, then are ye bastards, and not sons."* God, in his infinite wisdom and endless love, specifically and consistently disciplines His disobedient children *"for our [their] profit, that we [they] might be partakers of his holiness"* (Hebrews 12:10).

♥The Expansion of the Marriage Covenant♥

Hebrews 12:11-13 acknowledges that, *"Now no chastening for the present seemeth to be joyous, but grievous: nevertheless afterward it yieldeth the peaceable fruit of righteousness unto them which are exercised thereby. Wherefore lift up the hands which hang down, and the feeble knees; And make straight paths for your feet, lest that which is lame be turned out of the way; but let it rather be healed."* Christian parents who desire to represent God the Father will consistently discipline the sin of their children, recognizing that the benefit of the present, short-term sorrow is future, long-term obedience. They will quickly restore their children to a proper and joyous relationship following the correction through loving words of reassurance and a tender hug so that no long-term discouragement takes root and turns to bitterness.

♥ *Are we committed to biblically discipline our children so that they have a true understanding of right and wrong?*

♥ *Are we committed to always represent God the Father to our children through the manner and purpose of our discipline?*

♥ *Are we committed to always show proper forgiveness and restoration so that our children are secure in our love for them?*

Unity in Provision

Jesus Christ constantly provided for the needs and safety of his disciples. When they were hungry, He fed them, when they needed money to pay taxes, He provided for them, and when they found themselves in a storm, He protected them. Christian parenting should strive to give the same level of provision. Provision must be understood biblically. Provision is not the supply of every desire, but rather the supply of the necessities. Paul said it simply in I Timothy 6:7-8 when he said, *"For we brought nothing into this world, and it is certain we can carry*

nothing out. And having food and raiment let us be therewith content." Parents should not be concerned with always giving the newest and best to their children, but they should remember that "***if any provide not for his own, and specially for those of his own house, he hath denied the faith, and is worse than an infidel***" (I Timothy 5:8). Ultimately, parents should work together to provide, to the best of their ability, for the needs of their children. They then must depend on God by taking heed to Jesus's words as he said, "***Take no thought for your life, what ye shall eat, or what ye shall drink; nor yet for your body, what ye shall put on. Is not the life more than meat, and the body than raiment? Behold the fowls of the air: for they sow not, neither do they reap, nor gather into barns; yet your heavenly Father feedeth them. Are ye not much better than they? Which of you by taking thought can add one cubit unto his stature? And why take ye thought for raiment? Consider the lilies of the field, how they grow; they toil not, neither do they spin: And yet I say unto you, That even Solomon in all his glory was not arrayed like one of these. Wherefore, if God so clothe the grass of the field, which to day is, and to morrow is cast into the oven, shall he not much more clothe you, O ye of little faith? Therefore take no thought, saying, What shall we eat? or, What shall we drink? or, Wherewithal shall we be clothed? (For after all these things do the Gentiles seek:) for your heavenly Father knoweth that ye have need of all these things. But seek ye first the kingdom of God, and his righteousness; and all these things shall be added unto you***" (Matthew 6:25-33).

❤ *Are we committed to display our love for our children by providing what they need (not necessarily what they want)?*

❤ *Are we committed to trust God to provide for our needs and display this trust to our children as we supply their needs?*

❧Relationship Building Questions❦
Article IX

1. How many children do each of you desire to have?
   Husband _____ Wife _____

2. How can we display our dependence on God for our children?
   a. _____
   b. _____
   c. _____

3. How can we display our willingness to give our children back to God?
   a. _____
   b. _____
   c. _____

4. What are some ways that we might show that we are not unified in our child rearing?
   a. _____
   b. _____
   c. _____
   Who is to be the leader in raising children (Ephesians 6:4, Colossians 3:21)? _____

5. How can we prepare ourselves for raising godly children?
   a. _____
   b. _____
   c. _____

♥The Expansion of the Marriage Covenant♥

6. What are some important Christian character qualities that we must teach to our children.
   Provide a passage and a small example for each one.
   a. _____
   b. _____
   c. _____
   d. _____

7. What are some practical ways that we can teach our children God's Word?
   a. _____
   b. _____
   c. _____

8. What are the three responsibilities we have while disciplining their children?
   a. _____
   b. _____
   c. _____

9. What is the most common form of parental discipline presented throughout the Scriptures? _____

10. What does the Bible say parents do when they properly discipline their children? _____

11. Whose authority and love do Christian parents represent as they discipline their children? _____

12. What basic needs should we provide for our children?
    a. _____
    b. _____
    c. _____

Parental Counsel from King Solomon
"My Son"
Throughout Proverbs

Proverbs 1:8-9
8 **My son**, hear the instruction of thy father,
and forsake not the law of thy mother:
9 For they shall be an ornament of grace unto thy head,
and chains about thy neck.

Proverbs 1:10
10 **My son**, if sinners entice thee, consent thou not.

Proverbs 1:15-16
15 **My son**, walk not thou in the way with them;
refrain thy foot from their path:
16 For their feet run to evil,
and make haste to shed blood.

Proverbs 2:1-5
1 **My son**, if thou wilt receive my words,
and hide my commandments with thee;
2 So that thou incline thine ear unto wisdom,
and apply thine heart to understanding;
3 Yea, if thou criest after knowledge,
and liftest up thy voice for understanding;
4 If thou seekest her as silver,
and searchest for her as for hid treasures;
5 Then shalt thou understand the fear of the LORD,
and find the knowledge of God.

Proverbs 3:1-2
1 **My son**, forget not my law;
but let thine heart keep my commandments:
2 For length of days, and long life, and peace,
shall they add to thee.

Proverbs 3:11-12
11 **My son**, despise not the chastening of the LORD;
neither be weary of his correction:
12 For whom the LORD loveth he correcteth;
even as a father the son in whom he delighteth.

Proverbs 3:21
21 **My son**, let not them depart from thine eyes:
keep sound wisdom and discretion:

Proverbs 4:10
10 Hear, O **my son**, and receive my sayings;
and the years of thy life shall be many.

Proverbs 4:20-22
20 **My son**, attend to my words;
incline thine ear unto my sayings.
21 Let them not depart from thine eyes;
keep them in the midst of thine heart.
22 For they are life unto those that find them,
and health to all their flesh.

Proverbs 5:1-2
1 **My son**, attend unto my wisdom,
and bow thine ear to my understanding:
2 That thou mayest regard discretion,
and that thy lips may keep knowledge.

Proverbs 5:20-21
20 And why wilt thou, **my son**,
be ravished with a strange woman,
and embrace the bosom of a stranger?
21 For the ways of man
are before the eyes of the LORD,
and he pondereth all his goings.

Proverbs 6:1-5

1 **My son**, if thou be surety for thy friend,
if thou hast stricken thy hand with a stranger,
2 Thou art snared with the words of thy mouth,
thou art taken with the words of thy mouth.
3 Do this now, **my son**, and deliver thyself,
when thou art come into the hand of thy friend;
go, humble thyself, and make sure thy friend.
4 Give not sleep to thine eyes,
nor slumber to thine eyelids.
5 Deliver thyself as a roe from the hand of the hunter,
and as a bird from the hand of the fowler.

Proverbs 6:20-22

20 **My son**, keep thy father's commandment,
and forsake not the law of thy mother:
21 Bind them continually upon thine heart,
and tie them about thy neck.
22 When thou goest, it shall lead thee;
when thou sleepest, it shall keep thee;
and when thou awakest, it shall talk with thee.

Proverbs 7:1-3

1 **My son**, keep my words,
and lay up my commandments with thee.
2 Keep my commandments, and live;
and my law as the apple of thine eye.
3 Bind them upon thy fingers,
write them upon the table of thine heart.

Proverbs 19:27

27 Cease, **my son**, to hear the instruction
that causeth to err from the words of knowledge.

Proverbs 23:15

15 **My son**, if thine heart be wise,
my heart shall rejoice, even mine.

Proverbs 23:19
19 Hear thou, **my son**, and be wise,
and guide thine heart in the way.

Proverbs 23:26
26 **My son**, give me thine heart,
and let thine eyes observe my ways.

Proverbs 24:13-14
13 **My son**, eat thou honey, because it is good;
and the honeycomb, which is sweet to thy taste:
14 So shall the knowledge of wisdom be unto thy soul:
when thou hast found it,
then there shall be a reward,
and thy expectation shall not be cut off.

Proverbs 24:21-22
21 **My son**, fear thou the LORD and the king:
and meddle not with them that are given to change:
22 For their calamity shall rise suddenly;
and who knoweth the ruin of them both?

Proverbs 27:11
11 **My son**, be wise, and make my heart glad,
that I may answer him that reproacheth me.

Proverbs 31:2
2 What, **my son**? and what, the son of my womb?
and what, the son of my vows?
3 Give not thy strength unto women,
nor thy ways to that which destroyeth kings.
*From the mother of Lemuel

Chapter 10

Article X
The Fulfilment in the Marriage Covenant
Genesis 2:23-25

Adam and Eve lived together being *"both naked, the man and his wife, and were not ashamed"* (Genesis 2:25). Physical fulfilment in the Marriage Covenant comes from total openness and revelation of one's self emotionally, spiritually, mentally, and physically. Physical intimacy in marriage is not just an act, but an interaction. God has established intercourse to be the union of the husband's and wife's beings: emotionally, spiritually, mentally, and physically (Matthew 12:30). In the act of physical intimacy the husband and wife are both making themselves very vulnerable as well as accepting responsibility for the vulnerability of their spouse. This vulnerability must never be abused or disregarded. Therefore, it is very important that both the husband and the wife maintain a biblical view and obedience to their part of physical intimacy. It is very important to remember that if tension develops in this area of the relationship, the damage is always taken personally and is deeply felt.

God's Program for Physical Intimacy

The Marriage Covenant found in Genesis 2:23-24 provides a God-approved and blessed source of intimate pleasure, which is presented in verse 25. *"And they were both naked, the man and his wife, and were not ashamed."* This intimate pleasure should not bring guilt. The world offers these same pleasures outside of marriage. Proverbs 9:13-17 gives a clear description of the world's temptation for its pleasure as it describes the ways of a

♥The Fulfilment in the Marriage Covenant♥

"foolish woman." It says, *"A foolish woman is clamorous: she is simple, and knoweth nothing. For she sitteth at the door of her house, on a seat in the high places of the city, To call passengers who go right on their ways: Whoso is simple, let him turn in hither: and as for him that wanteth understanding, she saith to him, Stolen waters are sweet, and bread eaten in secret is pleasant."* The world offers the sweetness of secret sin and the allure of wrongful fulfilment. It offers *"the pleasures of sin for a season"* (Hebrews 11:25). But the pleasures of the world only last for a short time before the pain of guilt and shame is produced. Proverbs 9:18 concludes the description of the foolish woman's ways by saying, *"**But he knoweth not that the dead are there; and that her guests are in the depths of hell.**"* God's program for intimate pleasure is that it continues and even grows over the years. God has created each man and woman with the ability to feel pain and pleasure. These abilities were not created without purpose. Pain helps provide protection when there is something wrong, and pleasure is to be enjoyed God's way so that long-term pain is never experienced.

In Genesis 2:25, Adam and Eve provide a perfect (without sin) example of a husband and wife's intimacy. Adam and Eve never experienced the need for clothes nor was there any form of self-consciousness until sin entered their relationship. The same should be true for every husband and wife under God's Marriage Covenant. As they are pure before God and their spouse, there should be no reason for shame. They must each recognize that they were created exactly the way God wanted them to be created. God planned for them to be seen by their spouse just as Adam and Eve walked together in the Garden of Eden before they made aprons from leaves.

♥ *Are we committed to God's plan for physical intimacy and total open with in the marriage covenant?*

❤The Fulfilment in the Marriage Covenant❤

God's Blessing on Physical Intimacy

God's plan for sexual intimacy and the pleasure which is experienced between a man and woman while under the Marriage Covenant is fully condoned and encouraged by God. Hebrews 13:4 says, *"Marriage is honourable in all, and the bed undefiled: but whoremongers and adulterers God will judge."* Notice the stark contrast. God will judge all those who fulfill their sexual pleasure outside of marriage, BUT sexual intimacy and pleasure found in the BED of marriage between a husband and wife is HONOURABLE! It is honourable in ALL things. The freedom given to a husband and wife in their sexual intimacy is virtually without limit because it is UNDEFILED. A close reading of the book of Song of Solomon will reveal God's desire for a husband's and wife's relationship. Throughout the book the husband and wife talk of the beauty of each other's bodies, the pleasures they find while being intimate, and the longing to be reunited when apart. The book, in it's poetic form, specifically mentions some of the intimate pleasures they enjoyed. In chapter 7 verses 10 through 13 the bride gives a sample of their romance in her invitation to her groom when she says, *"I am my beloved's, and his desire is toward me. Come, my beloved, let us go forth into the field; let us lodge in the villages. Let us get up early to the vineyards; let us see if the vine flourish, whether the tender grape appear, and the pomegranates bud forth: there will I give thee my loves. The mandrakes give a smell, and at our gates are all manner of pleasant fruits, new and old, which I have laid up for thee, O my beloved."* God desires the sexual intimacy in marriage to be a fulfilling and exhilarating experience.

❤ *Do we believe that physical intimacy in the Marriage Covenant is approved of and blessed by God?*

❤The Fulfilment in the Marriage Covenant❤

God's Process for Physical Intimacy

God does not separate physical intimacy from the rest of the marriage relationship. It is an extension and added blessing to a well-maintained matrimony. For this reason, it is very important that each partner is constantly fulfilling their God-given roles in their Marriage Covenant. The husband who lovingly lives according to his knowledge of his wife and gives *"honour unto the [his] wife, as unto the weaker vessel"* will naturally develop a warm environment in which his wife will know his care and desire intimacy (I Peter 3:7). As well, the wife who honors her husband and who adorns herself with a *"meek and quiet spirit"* will find her husband attracted to her and desiring intimacy (I Peter 3:7). God has made it so that a husband who knows (loves) his wife through life will find that she wants to know him in sexual intimacy (love making). And a wife who honors (submits to) her husband will find that he wants to honor her in sexual intimacy (to handle like a precious vessel) (I Peter 3:1-7).

The husband and wife who strive to make every other area of their marriage closely unified will naturally find that their lives are constantly touching. Because they are under the Marriage Covenant they have no need to heed Paul's warning in I Corinthians 7:1 which says, *"It is good for a man not to touch a woman."* They have every right and good reason to touch and follow through with the natural results. Paul goes on to say, *"Nevertheless, to avoid fornication, let every man have his own wife, and let every woman have her own husband"* (I Corinthians 7:4). Sexual intimacy in marriage is based on the *"touch"* of a properly interwoven relationship and is always destroyed by the "clash" of an improperly frayed relationship.

❤ *Are we committed to live closely together in order to develop a daily relationship which naturally produces physical intimacy?*

♥The Fulfilment in the Marriage Covenant♥

God's Protection in Physical Intimacy

God has created mankind with the ability and desire to experience sexual intimacy. However, sin has destroyed God's perfect creation and program. Because of this, God has established that not only is marriage the place for sexual intimacy, it is also the protection from wrong intimacy. I Corinthians 7:1 and 2 say, *"Now concerning the things whereof ye wrote unto me: It is good for a man not to touch a woman. Nevertheless, to avoid fornication, let every man have his own wife, and let every woman have her own husband."* The word *"nevertheless"* presents the transitional statement and solution to fornication. The solution to fornication is a Biblical marriage. Verse 9 restates this thought when it says, *"But if they cannot contain, let them marry: for it is better to marry than to burn."* God does not want any individual to suffer or fall into temptation because of their desire for sexual intimacy. Rather, He presents a protective program through an honorable solution: marriage.

Proverbs 5:15-23 uses a poetic wording to present a clear command and warning as it says, *"Drink waters out of thine own cistern, and running waters out of thine own well. Let thy fountains be dispersed abroad, and rivers of waters in the streets. Let them be only thine own, and not strangers' with thee. Let thy fountain be blessed: and rejoice with the wife of thy youth. Let her be as the loving hind and pleasant roe; let her breasts satisfy thee at all times; and be thou ravished always with her love. And why wilt thou, my son, be ravished with a strange woman, and embrace the bosom of a stranger? For the ways of man are before the eyes of the LORD, and he pondereth all his goings. His own iniquities shall take the wicked himself, and he shall be holden with the cords of his sins. He shall die without instruction; and in the greatness of his folly he shall go astray."* Condemnation will always come for those who look for sexual pleasure outside of marriage. Solomon counseled his son to focus all of his passion and pleasure on *"the wife of his youth."* By doing so, a husband will avoid looking *"on a woman to lust after her"* and committing *"adultery with her in his heart"* (Matthew 5:28). As well, a wife must always reverence her husband by keeping him as her source of security and emotional fulfillment so that she is not distracted by another man (Proverbs 31:10-12, Ephesians 5:33). A husband and wife should find a warm, prepared haven from the attacks of sexual sin in each other's arms.

❤ *Are we committed to keep satisfying each others' need for physical intimacy within the marriage covenant?*

God's Frequency for Physical Intimacy

Because God designed man and woman to enjoy sexual intimacy, He also provided the correct relationship for these pleasures in the Marriage Covenant. Because God knows the strength of man's and woman's sexual needs, He instructs a married couple to **"Defraud ye not one the other, except it be with consent for a time, that ye may give yourselves to fasting and prayer; and come together again, that Satan tempt you not for your incontinency"** (I Corinthians 7:5). The word defraud presents the idea of unjustly withholding or refraining from something. God does not give a specific schedule for sexual intimacy, but He is very clear that it should take place as regularly as possible so as to avoid Satan's temptation. I Corinthians 7:3 and 4 begin the command found in verse 5 by saying, **"Let the husband render unto the wife due benevolence: and likewise also the wife unto the husband. The wife hath not power of her own body, but the husband: and likewise also the husband hath not power of his own body, but the wife."** A husband and wife should seek to fulfill the needs for sexual intimacy in the life of their partner. They are to be the only source of fulfilment and they should enjoy the privilege of being entrusted with and depended on for such a precious and personal need.

If sexual intimacy is not frequent, and if each partner does not seek to use their body (any or all of it), to please and satisfy the other's needs, Satan will have the opportunity to develop doubt about their love and honor for each other and destroy their relationship. However, as a husband seeks to fulfill his wife's needs, wishes, dreams, etc. in their sexual intimacy, he will find his wife fully secure in his love and honor of her. Likewise, as a wife seeks to fulfill her husbands needs, wishes, dreams, etc. in their sexual intimacy, she will find her husband fully secure in her submission to and honor of him.

❤ *Are we committed to keep our physical intimacy frequent so as to protect each other from temptation of other sexual sins?*

God's Plan for Physical Intimacy

Genesis 4:1 says, **"And Adam knew Eve his wife; and she conceived, and bare Cain, and said, I have gotten a man from the LORD."** How significant that the word *"knew"* is used to describe physical intercourse. God's desire is for a husband and wife to "know" each better because of their physical intimacy. In order for a husband and wife to truly know each other, they must explore each other and their desires while together experiencing the pleasure of it all. I Peter 3:7, while speaking to husbands says, **"Likewise, ye husbands, dwell with them according to knowledge, giving honour unto the wife, as unto the weaker vessel, and as being heirs together of the grace of life; that your prayers be not hindered."** A husband and wife must work together to better know how to fulfill this obligation in their physical unity. They must seek to "know" (I Peter 3:7) each other

♥The Fulfilment in the Marriage Covenant♥

as they know (Genesis 4:1) each other. For this to be accomplished, they must be willing to communicate and listen intently to each other's desires. Each spouse must be constantly observant to the other's responses and always ready to give of themselves to please the other. They must take time and energy to study their spouse so that they can learn how timing, touch, location, etc. all affect the pleasure received by their mate. A husband and wife should enjoy exploring together and communicating the results of their exploration. However, they must be careful to never let any disappointments or unfulfilled expectations become barriers in their relationship, but rather accept them as new details they have learned to better improve their next opportunity to be together.

♥ *Are we ready to take time to openly communicate our personal desires and experiences so that we can grow in our knowledge of each other?*

♥ *Are we committed to use the knowledge we gain to provide greater pleasure for each other in the future?*

Physical Intimacy Scale

Crass
Comfortable
Cold
Proverbs 7:5-27
I Corinthians 7:2-4
Hebrews 13:4
I Corinthians 7:5

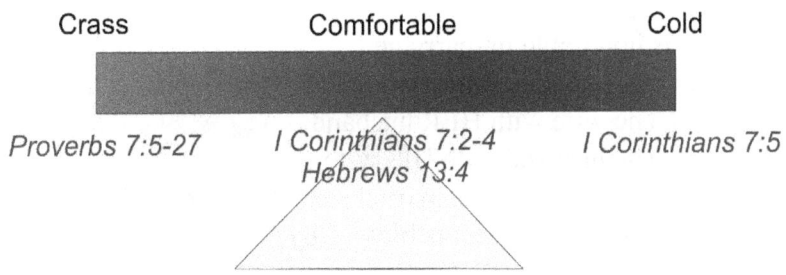

The P's of Proper Physical Intimacy

Including the Entirety of Man

Matthew 12:30

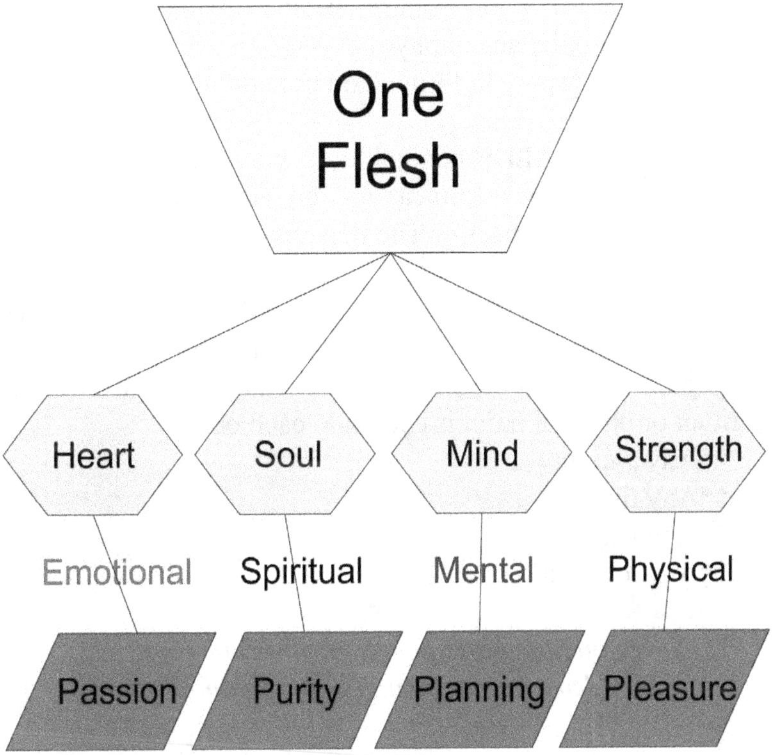

One
Flesh
Heart
Soul
Mind
Strength
Emotional
Spiritual
Mental
Physical
Passion
Purity
Planning
Pleasure

What is Honorable in Marriage
Hebrews 13:4

♡ <u>ALL</u> is honorable in marriage
   *The husband and wife relationship was established by God
      **The wife with HER husband
      **The husband with HIS wife
♡ <u>ALL</u> is pure in bed (the marital sexual intercourse)
   *The marital sexual act is blessed by God

❤ <u>NOTHING</u> is honorable in fornication nor adultery
   *Fornication - All sexual acts, before marriage, with another person, weather small or great, either by thought or by actual physical acts
   *Adultery - All sexual acts, during marriage, with another person that is not your spouse, weather small or great, either by thought or by actual physical acts
❤ <u>NOTHING</u> is pure in fornication nor adultery

*The question - If ALL is honorable and pure in the act of marital sex, but God judges fornication and adultery, what is the difference? The Practices or The Persons

*This verse offers COMPLETE FREEDOM en marital sexual intercourse with the only limitations being that only spouses participate with each other and that based on Biblical love, not spiritual or physical harm is caused to each other.
   **Any pleasure
   **Any time
   **Any way
   **Any location (private)

Never include other people in your marriage bed by videos, books, pictures, imagination ,etc.

*Sex is an adventure freely shared.
Completely enjoy exploring together.*

Tips for Intimacy

- Cleanliness aids in Closeness (Showers, fresh breath, etc. help to eliminate detractions.)
- Patience brings unified Pleasure (Taking time in the process helps to be sure everyone is prepared for the finale.)
- Grooming prevents Gouging (Shaving, nail clipping, etc. help to prepare smooth, soft skin rather than sandpaper and knives.)
- Soft Hands provide a Soft Touch (Lotions, oils, etc. can help to make sure that your skin is smooth and gentle.)
- Ambiance assists in Arousal (Sounds, smells, lighting, etc. all help to build or destroy romance.)
- Kindness kindles the Flame (Kind words, touches, actions, etc. throughout the day will help form a loving relationship for love making/expressing.)
- The Location can add to the Allure of adventure (Having a private but sometimes different location can help to build adventure and enjoyable memories for the future.)
- Positioning is Pivotal (Comfortable positions will help to provide pleasure rather than pain.)
- A "Quicky" Quenches while Time Taken Tarries (Providing a "quicky" can help keep the passion satisfied and produce anticipation for when more time and energy can be enjoyed.)
- Flirtation may build Desire (which is good) but Desire not realized produces Defrauding (which is bad.)

*Long periods of time should not be given to build anticipation for intimacy and proper communication and follow through must always be provided.

Illustrated Difference of Intimacy for a Man and a Woman

Men like the end result
(the faster and more aggressive the better)
Women like the process of getting there
(the slower and softer the better).

- Men are like jack in the boxes and women are like modeling clay.
- Men are like microwaves and women are slow cookers.
- Men work with bulldozers and women with feather dusters.
- Men like to drive quickly to arrive fast while women like leisurely strolls to arrive safely.

(These are not laws, simply general observations.)

Physical intimacy in marriage is like a jigsaw puzzle.
Each couple must work together
to line up every area of their relationship
to produce the beautiful picture found
in the physical one-flesh relationship of marriage.

Causes and Cures for Tension in Intimacy

1. Misunderstanding
   a. Physical intimacy between a husband and wife must never be thought of as dirty or cheap.
      i. God created it and said it was good (Genesis 1:26-31)
      ii. God blesses it with children (Genesis 1:28a, Psalms 127:3)
      iii. God said that it should be frequent (I Corinthians 7:1-5)
      iv. God said that it is "undefiled" (Hebrews 13:4)
   b. Physical intimacy between a husband and wife should be recognized as sharing, not just their bodies, but their entire being with each other. (Genesis 2:23-25)
   c. Physical intimacy should be anticipated and enjoyed by both parties. (Proverbs, 5:18-19, Song of Solomon)
   d. Physical intimacy should reveal each other's self-sacrificial love through patience and communication. (I Corinthians 7:3-5, 13:4-8, Ephesians 5:28-29, I Peter 3:7)

   *The practices of biblical love (I Corinthians 13:4-8) while making/expressing love will prove true love.
2. Past relationships
   a. Past relationships should never be a source of comparison to a biblical one-flesh relationship. (Proverbs 9:17-18, Hebrews 11:25b)
   b. Past relationships should have been totally revealed to each other so that no secret guilt can cause division. (Luke 8:17)
   c. Past relationships which have produced sin but have been confessed biblically should not be allowed to

destroy the acceptance of God's approval of and blessing on total sexual freedom provided within the husband and wife relationship (Proverbs 5:15-23, Hebrews 13:4).

Any sexual practices which were part of an unholy relationship should not be looked down on when now practiced within the one-flesh husband and wife relationship.

   d. Past relationships which were sinful must be seen as TOTALLY wrong and any fruit produced must be humbly accepted by both parties. (Galatians 6:7-8)
3. Lack of education (I Peter 3:7)
   a. Both the husband and wife should study to know the physical anatomy of their partner so that they can provide the most pleasure.

   When necessary, both the husband and wife should use educational materials to assist in understanding how God has designed them to enjoy their physical intimacy.

   Pornography must never be confused with educational material and will always bring damage to the relationship.

   b. Both the husband and wife must understand that the pleasure found in physical intimacy does not "just happen" like it is portrayed in the movies and books.

   Physical intimacy is like a jigsaw puzzle; it takes time, patience and intense desire to aline all the pieces correctly so that the beautiful picture, advertised picture can be revealed.

   c. Both the husband and wife must be willing to be vocally honest and revealing about their body and how their spouse can provide them pleasure.
   d. Both the husband and wife should be sure that they do not have any allergies to and are using correctly

any intimacy lotions, oils, etc. in order to prevent irritation or infections.
  e. Both the husband and wife must be willing to discuss any questions or concerns with a medical professional should the need should arise.
4. Frequency (I Corinthians 7:2-5)
  a. A husband and wife must accept that God has designed physical intimacy in marriage to be frequent so that temptation does not overtake either one.
     i. A husband and wife should pursue opportunities to enjoy their time of physical intimacy (Even if they need to schedule dates and times).
     ii. A husband or wife should never make false excuses for not being physically intimate with their spouse.

     Neither the husband nor the wife have authority over their own body but rather the authority over their body has been delegated to their spouse (vs. 4)

     iii. A husband or wife should be willing to provide "quickies" with and for each other when there is limited time or ability for more in order to satisfy the holy desire in order that Satan cannot tempt them with an unholy desire.
  b. A husband or wife must not put unrealistic expectations on each other based on their schedule, physical health, etc.

     The only biblical reason to not participate in physical intimacy is prayer and fasting when it is agreed on by both the husband and wife. (The amount of time stated in the Old Testament for spiritual cleansing which included no physical intimacy was three days - Exodus 19:15, I Samuel 21:4-6).

- c. A husband or wife must never withhold or use physical intimacy as a weapon for manipulation.
5. Unfulfilled expectations (Proverbs 13:12, I Corinthians 7:2-5)
    - a. A husband and wife must never accept the world's concept or advertisement of physical intimacy as reality.

        The world's and Satan's advertisement never reveals the whole truth. A proper physically intimate relationship is much more than just going to bed and letting "it" happen. It is work that lasts all day, and when accomplished in unity, provides the height of pleasure and unity.

        Pornography in books, pictures or video must never be a standard or stimulant for physical intimacy.
    - b. A husband and wife must find complete satisfaction in each other and understand that they are gifts from God specifically designed to provide the joy and pleasure He has planned for them. (Proverbs 5:15-23)
    - c. A husband and wife must never fall for the temptation of Satan that there is something better out there. Proverbs 9:17-18 is clear, *"Stolen waters are sweet, and bread eaten in secret is pleasant. But he knoweth not that the dead are there; and that her guests are in the depths of hell."*
    - d. A husband or wife may struggle with being adventurous while the other one is looking for more adventure. (I Corinthians 7:3-4, Hebrews 13:4)

        *Song of Solomon is a book that expresses great adventure in marital intimacy.
        - i. The spouse struggling with adventure must be sure that their apprehensions are not because of past guilt or shame, and that, in the Marriage

Covenant, there is nothing forbidden between a husband and wife.
   ii. The spouse struggling with adventure must remember that they are to try to provide their spouse with all the pleasure possible.
   iii. The spouse seeking adventure must be sure to defer to the conscience, wishes, feeling and true abilities of their spouse in order to show true love.
e. A husband and wife must guard themselves against taking personally any hesitation or the rejection of an intimate "advance" (I Corinthians 13:4-8).

Equally, a husband and wife must be cautious about hesitating or rejecting an advance by their spouse knowing that although they may have good cause in their mind, their spouse made the advance because they were interested in sharing themselves intimately no matter the circumstances (this rejection could be taken personally).

Sample
Charge to the Couple
&
Wedding Vows
Pastor Jeremy Markle

Jack and Jill, in accordance with your belief that God is the creator of the marriage relationship and the author of the Marriage Covenant, let us consider the first marriage established by God in the Garden of Eden as a model for each of your specific roles and responsibilities as you begin your new life together. In Genesis 2:7-8 the Bible records that, *"... the LORD God formed man of the dust of the ground, and breathed into his nostrils the breath of life; and man became a living soul. And the LORD God planted a garden eastward in Eden; and there he put the man whom he had formed."* God, on the 6th day of creation, created man from the dust of the ground and placed him in a perfect, and sinless environment. As He looked upon man, alone in the garden *"... the LORD God said, It is not good that the man should be alone; I will make him an help meet for him"* (Genesis 2:18) Although Adam was created perfectly in the image of God and possessed his own body, soul, and spirit, he was not complete. Adam needed someone special to be his companion and to complete his life. It is very significant that God did not create woman immediately. Instead Genesis 2:19-20 says, *"And out of the ground the LORD God formed every beast of the field, and every fowl of the air; and brought them unto Adam to see what he would call them: and whatsoever Adam called every living creature, that was the name thereof. And Adam gave names to all cattle, and to the fowl of the air, and to every beast of the field; but for Adam there was not found an help meet for him."* God had created Adam to fulfill a leadership role. He was in charge of all of creation. And by naming each animal, he was putting his leadership into practice. Adam was given the responsibility of naming the animals, he was given the opportunity to choose each name, and he was given the authority to follow through with his choice. But as Adam completed the task the Bible says, *"there was not found an help meet for him"* (Genesis 2:20b). God did not intend for Adam to find his companion among the animals or be completed by his labors. He had a much better plan.

Jack, today you stand in Adam's place. You have been created by God's hand with your own body, soul, and spirit but you are not complete without a help meet. Just as God did not provide Eve for Adam immediately after his creation God did not give you Jill immediately following your birth. God has had His own special plan for your life. He has given you responsibilities to fulfill so as to prepare you for this day and the leadership you will need to provide for Jill throughout the rest of your life. God also wants you to recognize that there is no other creature on this planet which can fulfill your need and not even your own labor will bring as much satisfaction to your life as when you are in a proper relationship with your bride.

Let us continue. After all the animals were created, and Adam had given each its name, Genesis 2:21-22 says, *"And the LORD God caused a deep sleep to fall upon Adam, and he slept: and he took one of his ribs, and closed up the flesh instead thereof; And the rib, which the LORD God had taken from man, made he a woman, and brought her unto the man."* Adam and all the animals were created directly from the ground, but this new creation was to be precious. It was to be created from Adam's very flesh and bone. God did not desire for Adam's help meet to be like any other created being. She was special, she was specifically created to be Adam's companion and completer, to walk by his side the rest of his life and assist him in every task he encountered from that day forward.

Jill, this is where your role is made clear. You have been created perfectly to fulfill your role as Jack's companion and completer. To be his helper in everything. To be by his side, offering friendship and assistance wherever God takes him and in whatever task God gives him.

Now, let us consider Adam's own words as he expresses his satisfaction with and commitment to the new relationship God established for him. He said, *"This is now bone of my bones, and flesh of my flesh: she shall be called Woman, because she was taken out of Man"* (Genesis 2:23). Adam, while fulfilling his role as the leader, gave his newly created help meet her name. He did not form a new name, but rather chose a name which was directly connected to his own so as to declare their personal and life-long connection to each other. He, in essence says, "this one is mine, no one else can have her, and I am going to let everyone know that she is mine by giving her a name which is directly connected to me."

Genesis 2:24 continues with, *"Therefore shall a man leave his father and his mother, and shall cleave unto his wife ..."* This statement is so very significant because Adam and Eve did not have human parents, yet it is clear: a husband's new relationship with his wife would change all other relationships and become the focus of his life. Husband and wife are inseparably bound together and become *"one flesh"* (Genesis 2:24b). In Matthew 19:6 Jesus Christ expounds on these words, and expressed God's view of the husband and wife relationship as He said, *"Wherefore they are no more twain, but one flesh. What therefore God hath joined together, let not man put asunder."* Jack and Jill, the marriage covenant which you are about to make together is permanent. No human power has the authority to terminate your relationship or relinquish your specific God-given roles.

Jack and Jill, just as God brought Adam and Eve together in the Garden of Eden on the 6th day of creation, today, by your presence in this place, you give testament to the fact that God has brought you both together to fulfill the biblical roles of husband and wife.

Jack, you are to be Jill's leader. A leader who guides based upon God's authority and in His love. Specifically Ephesians 5:25-28 says, *"Husbands, love your wives, even as Christ also loved the church, and gave himself for it; That he might sanctify and cleanse it with the washing of water by the word, That he might present it to himself a glorious church, not having spot, or wrinkle, or any such thing; but that it should be holy and without blemish. So ought men to love their wives as their own bodies. He that loveth his wife loveth himself."* You must follow Christ's example and self-sacrificially protect and provide for Jill in every area of life. Jill, you are to be Jack's help meet, a help meet who is a constant companion and faithful completer. Specifically Ephesians 5:22 says, *"Wives, submit yourselves unto your own husbands, as unto the Lord."* Submission is not slavery, but rather a self-sacrificial dedication to follow and help another individual. Jill, the authority to which you are to submit is not Jack's, but rather Jesus Christ's. In other words, you will display your submission to Jesus Christ as you submit to Jack. Verse 33 says it this way, *"and the wife see that she reverence her husband."* Jill, you are to honor and respect Jack's leadership so that you can both work together and glorify God in all you do.

Jack and Jill, the final verse of Genesis chapter 2 summarizes God's marriage covenant. Verse 25 says, *"And they were both naked, the man and his wife, and were not ashamed."* In a biblically based marriage, where God is at the center and the husband and wife properly fulfill their roles, there will be total transparency without shame. The husband and wife will always be united because of a loving respect for each other and a dedication to self-sacrificially fulfill each other's needs, all to the glory of God.

Pastor

Jack on this day, as God, being represented by the authority of Jill's father, has brought to you Jill to be your companion and completer in life, you must look upon her as Adam looked upon Eve and forsake all others in order to cleave unto her alone.

And so I ask you now before God and these witnesses, will you self-sacrificially love Jill by nourishing and cherishing her as if she were your own body? Will you work daily to better know her so that you can better honor her as the precious gift from God that she is? And will you protect her with all of your being and provide for her with all of your earthly goods?

Jack

I will

Pastor

Jill, as you stand along side Jack today, representing the way in which Eve was created from Adam's side, you must look upon him as your God given leader and forsake all others in order to cleave unto him alone.

And so I ask you now before God and these witnesses, will you submit to Jack's leadership both physically and spiritually? Will you reverence him as the head of your home? And will you walk by his side through all of life's circumstances as his faithful companion and confidante?

Jill

I will

Pastor

Jack and Jill, as you are prepared to express your dedication to faithfully love each other until death do you part, I desire to challenge you with the true meaning of the word "love." Although the world defines love as emotions or feelings which can change in a moment, God's Word describes love by using the word charity when it says ***"Charity suffereth long, and is kind; charity envieth not; charity vaunteth not itself, is not puffed up, Doth not behave itself unseemly, seeketh not her own, is not easily provoked, thinketh no evil; Rejoiceth not in iniquity, but rejoiceth in the truth; Beareth all things, believeth all things, hopeth all things, endureth all things. Charity never faileth..."*** The greatest display of such love is found in God's love for each of you. John 3:16 says, ***"For God so loved the world, that he gave his only begotten Son, that whosoever believeth in him should not perish, but have everlasting life."*** This verse does not mention emotion or feeling, but rather God's decision to sacrificially accomplish what is best for each person who will accept His love, by providing them with eternal life. Jesus said, ***"Greater love hath no man than this, that a man lay down his life for his friends"*** (John 15:13). In other words, love at its purest and most dedicated state is found when an individual is willing to sacrifice his belongings and even his own life for another. There is no greater example of such love than Jesus Christ's death on the cross for your sins. Romanos 5:8 explains by saying, ***"But God commendeth his love toward us, in that, while we were yet sinners, Christ died for us."*** Jill, based upon your personal testimony, I know that at the age of 8 you accepted God's love through your personal faith in the finished work of Jesus Christ on the cross. And Jack, based upon your personal testimony, I know that at the age of 12 you accepted God's love through your personal faith in the finished work of Jesus Christ on the cross. Now, at this moment, as you are about to make a life long covenant together, I challenge you with the Words of Jesus Christ as He said, ***"This is my commandment, That ye love one another, as I have loved you"*** (John 15:12). As God has freely offered his love to you, you both must be dedicated to sacrificially love one another for the rest of your lives.

Pastor

Recognizing the life-long commitment contained in the Marriage Covenant as well as your need to lovingly fulfill your God-given roles and responsibilities, are you prepared to enter into such a covenant before God and these witnesses at this time?

Bride & Groom
We are

Pastor
Jack Jones do you
in the presence of God and these witnesses,
and by a holy covenant,
solemnly pledge to Jill,
to honor her as one different in role, equal in Christ;
To provide, cherish and lead her;
And to encourage her in her spiritual walk.
To love her with all your being;
Always seeking to better know her;
Putting her good before your own;
Remaining faithful to her, forsaking all others,
Even unto death.

Groom
I do

Pastor
Jill Smith do you
in the presence of God and these witnesses,
and by a holy covenant,
solemnly pledge to Jack,
to submit to his leadership under Christ;
To reverence, encourage and help him;
And to be his partner in life in accordance to the Word of God.
To love him with all your being;
Always seeking his best interest;
Putting his good before your own;
Remaining faithful to him, forsaking all others,
Even unto death.

Bride
I do

Exchanging of Rings

Groom

I, Jack, take you, Jill,
To be my lawfully wedded wife,
to have and to hold from this day forward
for better and for worse,
for richer and for poorer,
To love and to cherish
until death do we part,
In accordance to God's holy Word
and with Christ at the center of our home.
I pledge thee my faithfulness
And with this ring,
I thee wed.

Bride

I, Jill, take you, Jack,
To be my lawfully wedded husband,
To have and to hold from this day forward
For better and for worse,
For richer and for poorer,
in sickness and in health,
to love and to cherish
until death do we part
In accordance to God's holy Word
and with Christ at the center of our home.
I pledge thee my faithfulness
And with this ring,
I thee wed.

Pronouncement of Couple

Jack and Jill, based upon the Marriage Covenant which you have entered into before God and these witnesses and have thereto confirmed by the giving and receiving of these rings; by the authority vested in me as a minister of the Lord Jesus Christ, and in accordance to the laws of the State of New Jersey, I pronounce you husband and wife. What God hath joined together, let not man put asunder.

!!Jack, you may now kiss your bride!!

Presentation of the Couple

It is now my privilege to congratulate and to introduce to you for the first time, on this the 23rd day of October 2010, Mr. & Mrs. Jack Jones.

A Heavenly Marriage Covenant
entered into on
the 20th of June, 2015

I, Jack, take you, Jill,
To be my lawfully wedded wife.
to have and to hold from this day forward
for better and for worse,
for richer and for poorer,
To love and to cherish
until death do we part,
In accordance to God's holy Word
and with Christ at the center of our home.
I pledge thee my faithfulness
And with this ring,
I thee wed.

I, Jill, take you, Jack,
To be my lawfully wedded husband,
To have and to hold from this day forward
For better and for worse,
For richer and for poorer,
in sickness and in health,
to love and to cherish
until death do we part
In accordance to God's holy Word
and with Christ at the center of our home.
I pledge thee my faithfulness
And with this ring,
I thee wed.

_____
Jack Smith

_____
Jill Schmidt

Jack and Jill,
based upon the Marriage Covenant which you have entered into before God and these witnesses
and have thereto confirmed by the giving and receiving of these rings;
by the authority vested in me as a minister of the Lord Jesus Christ, and in accordance to the laws of the State of New Jersey,
I pronounce you husband and wife.
What God hath joined together, let not man put asunder.

_____
Pastor Jeremy Markle

Other Ministry Resources Available From Walking in the WORD Ministries

Parenting with Purpose seeks to help young parents to spiritually prepare for the great privilege they have to care for and guide the life of one of God's precious creations. The first three lessons focus on the parents' need to honor God with their child, while the final three lessons focus on the parents' opportunity to represent God the Father to their child.

Missions: Ministering Beyond Our Borders was written to provide insight into the physical, emotional, and spiritual adjustments a missionary faces as he begins his new life and ministry. Throughout its pages you will find spiritual encouragements for the missionary and helpful hints for his family and friends who desire to support him in his service to their Lord and Savior Jesus Christ. There is also "Missionary Edition" which provides a large appendix with additional tips specifically for missionaries.

The Deputation Trail: Ministry or a Means to an End? was written to help missionaries during their pre-field ministry by presenting biblically-based philosophies and practical tips to guide them through a God-honoring, church-expanding, and believer-edifying, deputation ministry.

www.walkinginthewordministries.net

Los Otros Estudios Bíblicos y Libros
disponible por
Los Ministerios de Andando en la PALABRA
www.walkinginthewordministries.net

**Matrimonio:
Un Pacto Delante de Dios**
Diez estudios y materiales extras
para ayudar a una pareja
tener un matrimonio bíblico.

La Crianza con Propósito
Seis estudios
sobre la crianza bíblica.
Los primeros tres estudios se enfoquen en la necesidad de los padres
de honrar a Dios con su niño.
Los últimos tres estudios se enfoquen en cómo los padres tienen que representar Dios Padre a su niño.

**La Armadura de Dios para las Batallas Diarias
Una Guía de Bosquejo para El Camino del Calvario**
de Roy Hession
**La Búsqueda para la Mano de Dios en Mi Vida
El Corazón del Hombre
¿Qué dice la Biblia sobre:
La Salvación?, El Bautismo?, La Membresía de la Iglesia?
¿Quiénes Son Los Bautistas? Según Sus Distintivos
¿La Voluntad de Dios es un Rompecabezas para Ti?
Los Componentes Básicos para una Vida Cristiana Estable**

www.ingramcontent.com/pod-product-compliance
Lightning Source LLC
Chambersburg PA
CBHW061944070426
42450CB00007BA/1051